MALASPINA & GALIANO

MALASPINA & GALIANO

Spanish Voyages to the Northwest Coast

1 7 9 1 & 1 7 9 2

DONALD C. CUTTER

Douglas & McIntyre
Vancouver/Toronto

University of Washington Press
Seattle

Douglas & McIntyre Ltd.
1615 Venables Street, Vancouver, British Columbia V5L 2H1

Canadian Cataloguing in Publication Data

Cutter, Donald C.
   Malaspina and Galiano

   Includes bibliographical references.
   ISBN 0-88894-715-1

   1. Malaspina, Alessandro, 1754–1809—Journeys--Northwest Coast of
North America. 2. Alcalá-Galiano, Dionisio, 1760–1805—Journeys—
Northwest Coast of North America. 3. Northwest Coast of North America—
Description and travel. 4. Northwest Coast of North America—Discovery
and exploration—Spanish. 5. Spain—Exploring expeditions. 6. Indians of
North America—Northwest Coast of North America. 7. Sutil (Ship) 8.
Mexicana (Ship)
I. Title.
F851.5.C87 1991   917.9504'2   C91-091045-6

Editing by Brian Scrivener
Design by Alexandra Hass
Printed and bound in Canada by D. W. Friesen & Sons Ltd.
Printed on acid-free paper ∞

Published simultaneously in the United States of America by
The University of Washington Press, PO Box 50096, Seattle,
Washington 98145-5096

Library of Congress Cataloging-in-Publication Data

Cutter, Donald C.
   Malaspina and Galiano : Spanish voyages to the Northwest Coast,
   1791 and 1792 / Donald C. Cutter
        p.   cm.
   Includes bibliographical references and index.
   ISBN 0-295-97105-3
   1. Malaspina, Alessandro, 1754–1809—Journeys—Northwest Coast of
North America. 2. Alcalá-Galiano, Dionisio, 1760–1805—Journeys—
Northwest Coast of North America. 3. Northwest Coast of North America—
Discovery and exploration--Spanish. 4. Seafaring life—Spain—History—18th
century. 5. Indians of North America—Northwest Coast of North America
6. Spaniards—Northwest Coast of North America—History—18th century.
7. Spain—Exploring expeditions. I. Title.
F851.5.C93   1991   90-50989
917.9504'2—dc20

*This work has been published as a companion book to the
exhibition "Enlightened Voyages: Malaspina and Galiano on the
Northwest Coast, 1791–1792," presented at the Vancouver Maritime
Museum in 1991. The publisher gratefully acknowledges the support
and assistance of the museum in making this publication possible.*

Contents

Preface

Many years ago Alejandro Malaspina first came to my attention as a little-known explorer who in 1791 had visited the isolated Spanish frontier province of California for a fortnight. I knew little more than the few remarks about his visit contained in standard works on California. In 1959 a bibliophile colleague brought to my attention a brief excerpt of the journal that had been published in the California Historical Society *Quarterly* in 1924. He encouraged me to do an amended and annotated translation that would find publication in a limited edition. I was at the point of departure for a sabbatical leave in Spain and I felt that a few well-spent weeks of that time would result in a modest but welcome publication.

Once immersed in the extant documentation, I quickly realized that there was a much larger story to be told than I had anticipated, but I hardly realized that off and on for the next thirty years I would be involved with the Italian-born navigator who led Spain's most ambitious naval scientific exploring expedition. My first efforts resulted in a book, *Malaspina in California*.

In the intervening years between those first efforts and today, much new material emanating from the 62-month-long cruise of the Spanish naval Corvettes *Descubierta* and *Atrevida* has come to light. By 1991, the bicentennial of the expedition's visit to the Pacific Coast, the dimensions of Malaspina's contribution are better known, as additional important artifacts and documents have become available. The companions who sailed with Malaspina on his long voyage are now better identified and their role in Spanish naval history is clearer. The present book focuses on the Malaspina expedition's visit to the Pacific Northwest Coast of North America. In addition to the story of Spanish exploration, recent historical, anthropological, geographical and natural scientific studies have permitted enrichment of the

Malaspina story, a tale filled with adventure, hard work and dedication, one crowned by the thrill of discovery and doomed to an ultimate tragic end.

Over the decades I have become debtor to many individuals while following in the wake of Malaspina. The successive directors of the Museo Naval – Julio Guillén, Luis Morales, José María Zumalácarregui – were generous contributors. The present director, Admiral Vicente Buyo Couto, and my longtime friend and director of the Museo de América, Dr. Juan González Navarrete, have been particularly instrumental in the formation of this book.

Others who merit special mention in Spain as colleagues in the Malaspina effort and who have been constant sources of help have been Lola Higueras, María Luisa Martín-Merás and Pilar San Pío, all of the Museo Naval. Mercedes Palau, of the Spanish Comisión Quintocentenario del Descubrimiento de América, has long been involved in our shared knowledge of Malaspina. In the United States, Iris Wilson Engstrand of the University of San Diego and I have followed Malaspina from midshipman to rear admiral.

To my friends in British Columbia who have spurred my present interest, I owe a debt of gratitude – Robin Inglis, Director of the Vancouver Maritime Museum, John Kendrick and Freeman Tovell – all of whom have shared in efforts to revive Malaspina and to applaud the work of that early naval scientist. Most important of my collaborators has been Charlotte Lazear Cutter, my wife, who has integrated the Malaspina effort into our existence, who has helped materially in research, and who has provided wise and helpful counsel.

In the present study I have attempted to maintain a general chronological narrative with some necessary digressions. There is little attempt to present any original contribution to regional ethnography. Instead, I attempt to tell in some detail the Malaspina story as it unfolded from May to August 1791, and again with the smaller subunit in the summer of 1792. In great measure I recount their activity as they recorded it, including their comments on Indian life as seen by late-eighteenth-century natural scientists. In a brief four months following departure from Acapulco until return from Nootka Sound on the west coast of Vancouver Island, a surprisingly extensive amount of investigation was carried out. However, time was too short in 1791 to do all that had been desired and ordered by higher authority. A second visit by a subgroup led by expedition officers Dionisio Alcalá Galiano and Cayetano Valdés was made in the summer of 1792 to complete the unfinished business. As early visitors to the area, both groups influenced place name geography by direct and indirect contributions. In the latter case, Alcalá Galiano has been reduced to simply Galiano, clearly a non-Spanish rendering of his surname.

As scientists, the Spanish visitors to the Northwest made their more lasting contributions in the fields of anthropology and history. Their eighteenth-century work in other fields, such as cartography, geography, astronomy, physics, botany and zoology, has been made obsolete by subsequent activities. But the men of the *Descubierta* and *Atrevida* not only were recorders of events; they also became participants in the area's story. Before the discipline of anthropology was identified as such, members of the expedition became close observers and recorders of two native cultures of the Pacific Northwest. They became collectors of some of the earliest artifacts extant from those areas, and even became modest precursors in the study of linguistics. Although Pacific Northwest Coast cultures were never static, the early natural scientists' views do serve as a frame of reference for establishing what Tlingit and Nootka culture were like near the time of first contact with the White man.

MALASPINA & GALIANO

A Voyage of Enlightenment

About midday on 27 June 1791, a colourful event took place nearly five kilometres offshore from Port Mulgrave in Yakutat Bay, Alaska. Two identical Spanish naval vessels were intercepted by a pair of a tiny Tlingit Indian canoes racing at great speed and closing on the huge ships. The record the Spaniards left describes the event.

The first view, when they were near, was one of great astonishment, both for the Indians and for us; for the Indians because they did not cease looking at the ships, although they advised us and we soon verified that these were not the first ships that they had seen; for us, because such strange and marvelous subjects presented themselves to our sight. [To the visitors, the natives seemed exotic indeed]: They were dressed in skins of various colours, well-tanned, large and flexible. With one which hangs from a skin tied around their waist, they cover their private parts and the other which reaches to the knees they hang from their shoulder like a cape. The skins seem to be of bears, tigers, lions [sic], some of deerskins, and of marmots, with the hair to the outside. Their aspect would not be so disagreeable, although always wild, but the crude colours with which they paint themselves disfigure them entirely, as it seems that their idea of gala dress is to make themselves look as horrible as possible. Their hair is very thick and flaccid, without any dressing or care, loose in a carefree, natural manner, and covered with the greatest abundance of red ochre and grease, which according to the odour must be deer grease.

As soon as they were close to the ladder, all except the steersman stood up, and at the sound of a stentorian and frightful voice which the ugliest one, who was in the centre, uttered, they all extended their hands at the same time with great violence in the form of a cross, and turning their heads to one side intoned a very sad song in their language, which, however, preserved tune and time.[1]

The Spanish visitors, taken aback by some thirty lightly-clad warriors, by their songs noteworthy for both harmony and cadence, and by

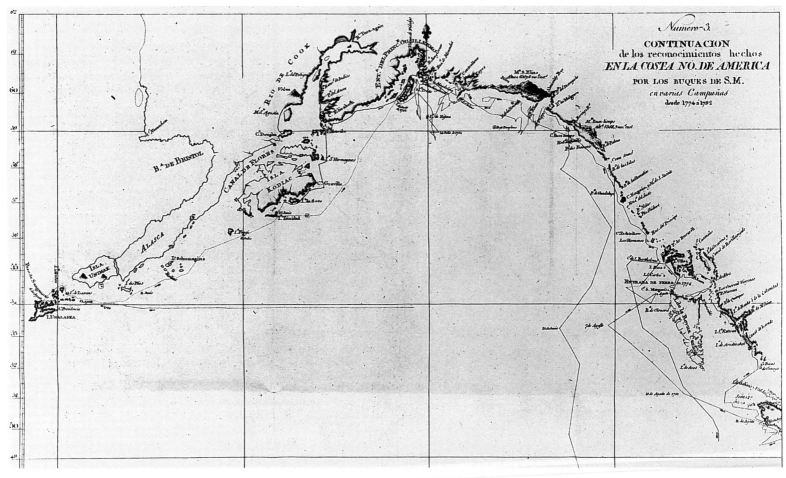

Spherical chart of the explorations on the Northwest Coast of America between 57° and 60°30' N, 1791. The anchorage at Mulgrave is shown, with the tracks of the Descubierta *and* Atrevida *in the shadow of Mount St. Elias. (Museo Naval IIB (7); Higueras 1723)*

their obvious signs of peace, attempted reciprocation by imitating those friendly actions. It was an auspicious start of Spanish-Indian relations, but just who were these visitors in their large vessels? What did they want? And why did the Tlingit Indians greet them so fearlessly?

The two Spanish vessels were the specially built Corvettes *Descubierta* and *Atrevida* which, immediately following their launch on 8 April 1789 at La Carraca shipyard and a brief shakedown cruise, had left the royal Spanish naval station at Cádiz in midsummer of that year. Carefully and expressly fabricated for an exploratory mission, each was of 306 tons burden. They had been constructed by a well-known naval shipbuilder, Tomás Muñoz, to specifications clearly outlined by the Spanish Naval Ministry. Not heavily-armed, possessing only sufficient fire power for self-defense, the vessels had been built for the primary mission of carrying out wide-ranging, detailed and complicated scientific studies. Many of the officers aboard had been hand-picked from among the cream of Cádiz Naval Academy graduates of recent vintage, selected to represent a variety of specialties. Even the original enlisted personnel were chosen with care. None were to be over thirty-five years old, nor were any to be under twenty. Within these limits, consideration was given to special characteristics of stamina and seamanship, particularly in handling of small boats. To this end, crew members were at first recruited from the northern Spanish provinces of Viscaya, Asturias and La Montaña, since it was believed that they would be able to endure better the cold weather. Of the initial goal of eighty, only sixteen were found there, disappointing in view of the projected normal complement of 86 men and 16 officers aboard each vessel.

The sudden appearance off their coast of two vessels, each 36 metres long and drawing a normal load displacement of 4.2 metres, must have come as a surprise to the Tlingits, who had seldom before seen European ships. Four years earlier, British mariner George Dixon had visited the same Yakutat Tlingit, and the new visitors had available a published report of that explorer's 1787 visit, which contained a map upon which some local place names appeared.[2] The Spanish visitors maintained those toponyms, including the name of the anchorage area, which Dixon had given in honour of Lord of the British Admiralty and Second Baron Mulgrave, Constantine John Phipps.

In command of the two-vessel Spanish task group were two career naval officers who had earlier presented to the naval ministry a cherished plan for circumnavigation of the globe as a contribution to the advancement of scientific knowledge. Two precedents seem to have motivated Captains Alejandro Malaspina and José Bustamante y Guerra. One was to emulate, or ideally surpass, the achievements of Captain Cook, whose exploits had found a substantial audience not only in Britain but also elsewhere in Western Europe. The commanders of the Spanish naval scientific expedition knew of and were guided by the earlier activities of Cook. They were also eager to exceed the lesser known achievements of Jean François Galaup de Lapérouse, who attempted for France what they were doing for Spain and what Cook had done for Great Britain. All were imbued by the spirit of the Age of the Enlightenment with a noble obligation to advance science by exploration of the little known parts of the world.

A second motive for the Spaniards was to duplicate, with greater emphasis on scientific inquiry, an earlier circumnavigation that Malaspina had accomplished in 1784 as captain of the Spanish naval vessel *Astrea*. In their initial proposal, the young captains had suggested a four-year period for their cruise, but as things turned out the voyage lasted slightly more than five years, in part due to unexpected circumstances that placed the Pacific Northwest Coast on their itinerary. Even so, the circumnavigation did not materialize, although in actual sailing distance it would have been easier and closer to return on their homeward bound voyage via the Cape of Good Hope than by retracing their outward bound Pacific crossing and returning by way of Cape Horn, which is what the expedition eventually did.

At some indeterminate time, the concept of dual command gave way to the enterprise being called the Malaspina expedition rather than the Malaspina-Bustamante voyage. Even before departure from Cádiz in 1789, some such references were made, perhaps because Malaspina was the elder of the two commanding officers. Malaspina was also the more vocal and motivated leader, though each continued to command his own corvette, with neither being considered the flagship of the task group. When they parted company for separate short-term missions, there was never any idea that Bustamante was in a subordinate capacity. Letters written as matters of protocol were customarily signed or at least sent in the name of both men. But the leadership of Malaspina had already become fully evident before the 1791 visit to Alaska and Canada.

Of the two commanders, Malaspina led a more dramatic life. He was born not in Spain but in Mulazzo in the Duchy of Parma in what is today Italy, but this was neither a great liability nor an asset. At the time that he assumed command of the *Descubierta*, no mention was made of his origins, perhaps because Parma, being under Spanish protection, was almost considered an integral part of Spain at a time when any concept of an Italy was still in the distant future. Malas-

pina's origin presented no problem when on 18 November 1774 he entered naval service as the result of a royal order of eleven days earlier. Alejandro did not attend Spain's Midshipmen's School at Cádiz but was rather assigned to serve in the Naval Department of Cartagena. He had all the requirements – he was of noble blood on all four grandparental sides. His parents were titled nobility and, had he been the eldest son, Alejandro would have been in line to inherit both ancestral titles and lands. The laws of primogeniture worked against him, though his elegant manners and bearing, and his well-developed sense of courtesy and dignity, early marked him as a man who could succeed.

Malaspina's rise to military prominence was rapid and his commissioned service was marked by various assignments associated with the Naval Department of Cádiz and with its midshipmen's training school and observatory. It was there that Malaspina became acquainted with most of the officers who later served under his command. In the years before departure, Malaspina apparently "spun a song of the sea" to many, for all who left with him on the grand cruise went as volunteers. During the expedition, Malaspina did his utmost to see that members of his staff were given prompt consideration for promotion, and in retrospect, it is evident that his recommendations, though sent from the distant corners of the globe, had their intended positive influence. These quick promotions were likewise a clear reflection of considerable royal and ministerial interest in the expedition's progress.

Malaspina was not the only expedition officer who was not of strictly Spanish origin. As subordinates he had Fabio Ali Ponzoni, a midshipman born at Cateneo on the Italian peninsula, and another part "Italian" was Juan Vernacci y Retamal. Also serving was Ensign

Jacobo Murphy y Connan, whose father was from Waterford, Ireland, and who was an asset in that he knew English. None were ever considered as other than regular naval officers.

Also on board were Dr. Tadeo Haenke, a Bohemian natural scientist, the Parmesans Fernando Brambila and Juan Ravenet who joined the expedition as artists just after the Pacific Northwest operation, and Luis Née, the expedition's botanist.

Commanding officer of the Corvette *Atrevida* was José Bustamante y Guerra, who despite Malaspina's protestations of equality between the two captains, early acknowledged that his associate was "chief of the expedition."[3] Captain Bustamante was a career naval officer born at Ontaneda in the mountainous northern Spanish province of Santander. He had become a midshipman at Cádiz in 1770. His subsequent rise to naval prominence matched that of Malaspina, and they apparently had served together and worked together prior to this voyage.

An obvious question arises concerning why an expedition of the magnitude proposed by Malaspina and Bustamante would be approved in the late 1780s. In the latter part of the eighteenth century, Spain was ruled for nearly two decades by Carlos III, fifth son of Felipe V, and formerly Duke of Parma. His rule coincided with a period of progress and recovery of lost national prestige. French influence on Carlos III brought closer contact with Northern Europe and with the Enlightenment. An exceedingly active monarch, one interested in recuperation of Spain's diminished position in European affairs, he dedicated himself to needed reform in commerce, agriculture, industry, architecture and science. In an age of scientific advance, he wanted Spain to match the efforts of rival nations in exploration and discovery. He was the moving spirit in implementing scientific

Alejandro Malaspina (1754-1810). Modern oil painting by Sebastián Cortés based on earlier portraits. (Vancouver Maritime Museum)

José Bustamante y Guerra (1753-1824), as captain of the Atrevida, *shared command with Malaspina, though the latter was the acknowledged "chief of the expedition." From an anonymous portrait. (Museo Naval A-1475; Higueras 3247)*

expeditions to study Spain's imperial holdings, and most had been successes. The Malaspina expedition was the last of a series of great explorations under the aegis of the enlightened rule of Carlos III, though it actually began after his death in 1788.

Under Carlos III's inept son, Carlos IV, both enthusiasm for exploration and support for reform slowly dwindled, yet favourable notice of Cook's explorations, as well as widespread interest in Lapérouse's activities and in his as yet unknown fate, were stimuli to Spanish activity. Some have ungenerously considered this concerted exploratory activity to have been nautical knight-errantry. Others have considered it imperialism in the guise of science, laying claim to leftover portions of the globe. More maturely, it can be viewed as the birth of modern scientific investigation in the unknown areas of the world, observation done for the benefit of man in an international quest for knowledge. Spain was playing its part by sending the Malaspina expedition, though it would be naïve to believe that altruism was the primary motivating force. Domestic political considerations played an important role in early phases of the voyage, while international relations were an overlying cause for the visit to northern latitudes.

At the time of departure from Spain in 1789, there had been no intention of going anywhere in the Pacific north of Hawaii. Those islands, the Sandwich Islands of Cook, had been visited by him and later by Lapérouse. The island chain was of some interest to Spain as a possible stopping place in the long-standing China trade. Malaspina's expedition had originally intended three months or more of exploration and mapping of the Hawaiian archipelago, a stay that might have had considerable influence on the history of those islands. Although Spanish tradition, and even some inconclusive evidence, suggests an Iberian discovery of Hawaii prior to that of Cook, Spain's slavish dedication to a northern great circle return route from Manila to Acapulco and her equal insistence on a straight shot from Acapulco to the Philippines had deprived her for over two hundred years of possible effective discovery of the gem of the Pacific.

Interest in the North Pacific resulted from rumours reaching Madrid by way of diplomatic sources in St. Petersburg indicating growing Russian interest in discovery and exploration out of Siberia eastward to the North American continent, as well as in visits to its offshore islands. These rumours, based on little-known facts of official and unofficial Russian visits to Alaska, proved to be true. When passed to Mexico City, these reports stimulated the Visitor General to New Spain, José de Gálvez, to combat such a potential threat. His first move was establishment of a small naval base and shipbuilding facility at San Blas on the Nayarit coast near the mouth of the Rio Santiago. This naval station became home base for a small fleet and its crews, units that were built up rapidly as circumstances required. Ship construction was begun, and officers sent from Spain were soon added to the local staff.

From San Blas in 1769, ships joined with overland parties to occupy Alta California, now the state of California. The success in establishment of Spanish control over an extended coastal area led to the beginning of naval exploration northward, beginning in 1774 with the *Santiago* under Juan Pérez. His initial expedition sailed as far as 55° north latitude but found no trace of Russian activity and failed to formally establish claim by performing an act of sovereignty.

Subsequent exploration followed to remedy this earlier oversight. In 1775-76, two vessels under Bruno de Hezeta, the *Santiago* and the *Sonora*, continued the voyages of discovery. Other nations and other Spaniards added to these early reconnaissances. All the while, Spain maintained a stance of exclusive sovereignty not only over the coast north of California, but also to the entire Pacific Ocean, basing its pretensions on ancient Papal Bulls and on a magnificent act of possession performed in 1514 by Vasco Núñez de Balboa in the Darien area of Panama. It was in defense of this policy of Spanish sovereignty over the entire length of the Pacific Coast that successive exploratory expeditions were sent northward from the new naval base at San Blas.

The almost instant success of the California colonization project and the frequent use of San Blas vessels to support that operation brought about dual utilization of those ships – logistic support of the new colony and exploration of the coasts beyond. The second concept resulted in both expansion and international involvement. In 1789 Spain determined to occupy the north coast by establishing a military outpost at Friendly Cove in Nootka Sound on what is now called Vancouver Island. A small army detachment, a breastwork of earth, rock and timbers, and a supporting settlement were nestled into a sheltered cove which up to that time had been Yuquot, a Nootkan coastal village under the local principal chief, Maquinna. The zealous though imprudent naval officer in charge was Lieutenant Estevan José Martínez, a Sevillian mariner of greater experience than judiciousness. Two of his early actions had important consequences. The first was his responsibility for the shooting death of Nootka subordinate chief Callicum, which resulted in strained relations between the Nootkans and the Spaniards. The second notorious act was his capture of two British merchant vessels that were at Nootka in 1789 under Captain James Colnett. The seizure set off the Nootka Sound Controversy, a slow-burning international incident that by the time of Malaspina's arrival in the area had not yet been settled. When a final solution was eventually reached, it had little to do with the merits of the case and a great deal to do with the status of European diplomatic and military affairs. Since the final outcome of the controversy is unimportant to Malaspina's 1791 visit or to that of his subordinates in 1792, no attempt will be made to describe those dealings. However, it was in great measure in pursuit of Spanish policy regarding Nootka that his naval scientific exploration was diverted from an anticipated pleasant Hawaiian stay and sent in the late spring of 1791 to the far north. Although this detour was mostly for political reasons, science was served notwithstanding the change in itinerary.

Despite earlier northern explorations, the long-standing question of the existence of a strait leading from the North Sea to the South Sea, that is, between the Atlantic and Pacific Oceans, had not yet been answered. A resolution was important to Spain, though a negative result might have served Spanish national interests better than a positive one. Fanciful map makers left room for the as yet unextinguished possibility of a navigable strait through North America. European nations had some vague reasons to believe that one existed, with the British making the greatest efforts to find a practicable Northwest Passage. The Spanish version, more susceptible of approach from the west than from the east, was known as the Strait of Anian, though at times other names were applied to the mythical waterway. The Strait of Admiral Bartolomé Fonte, the Strait of Lorenzo Ferrer Maldonado and the Strait of Juan de Fuca were among the names used and occasionally placed on early maps, cartographic representations that led mariners astray in their judgement.

Although at the time of the Malaspina expedition there was serious doubt about a strait in northern waters, there was still a remote chance that one existed. If it did, the nation seizing the entrance and thereby controlling that waterway would hold significant advantage. It was felt that a well-equipped, well-directed expedition, the Malaspina group, could solve the puzzle once and for all time, a matter of great national importance to Spain.[4]

Preparations for the Voyage

The Malaspina expedition recognized that the best source of information on Pacific Northwest navigation was the experienced commandant of the Department of San Blas, Captain Juan Francisco de la Bodega y Quadra. As early as 1775, Bodega had been in those northern waters. By 1791, he was a senior officer and had access to copies of the journals of all officers who had been on the coast. On 15 April, while the *Atrevida* was in port at his naval station, Bodega wrote for the scientific expedition's guidance a "Course that I conjecture would be proper for the Commanders of the Descubierta and Atrevida to observe on the Northern Coast of California to eliminate the doubts that up to the present we have, and to make a map of it." Bodega's treatise gives California the elastic limits of the late eighteenth century, meaning anything to the north of Cape San Lucas at the tip of Lower California. His lengthy advice first warned of the need for ships to clear the coast by swinging westward and even somewhat south to avoid unfavourable sailing conditions, pick up favourable winds, and follow them along courses in the fourth quadrant (between 270° and 360°), until reaching 37° north latitude and 38° west of San Blas.[5]

Experience showed that, at about that distant location, the winds shifted to the 2nd and 3rd quadrant, and by following them, sailing northnorthwest more or less along the 40th meridian, one would hit the northwest coast of America near Cape St. Elias, situated in 59° 54' north, and recognizable by the nearby great mountain perennially covered with snow from its crest to its slopes. By steering eastsoutheast, following the coast as far as the Bahía de Bering at 59° 18' north and 36° 48', it would not be difficult for the Spaniards to take possession nor to land and make astronomical observations. Bodega indicated that the coast should be followed closely in order to examine minutely all the inlets, capes and ports as far as that of Bucareli, where a second series of celestial observations should be taken. It would not be necessary to linger any longer there since by the time Malaspina arrived the area would already have been explored by San Blas vessels.

From Bucareli Bay, it was suggested that a route be taken between the Island of San Carlos and the mainland to as far as the Entrada de Pérez in 55°. Bodega favoured passing through the strait formed between the Isla de Florida Blanca and the mainland, and examining the inlet that stretches between Punta de Santiago and that of Boiset to perfect this exploration and to ascertain the existence or nullity of the Strait of Ferrer Maldonado.

From that last point on the coast the scientists were advised to steer southward between 101 and 113 degrees so as to hit the Port of Nootka, located in 49° 36' north and 22° 10' west, according to Cook, where a third observation should be made.

Bodega indicated that since it was very probable that on arriving at Nootka "you will find that they have already drawn up its map and found out if it is on an island, as is believed, the amount of time that you will have to stay there will be little, so you will continue your course south."

Juan Francisco Bodega y Quadra (1744-1794) had made two voyages to the Northwest Coast in the 1770s. He assisted the expedition's preparations before Malaspina left San Blas. Oil painting by Julio García Condoy. (Maritime Museum of British Columbia)

He appended a series of warnings concerning the proposed navigation. Among these were:

From 41° to 45° you will see rough waters and will see various signs indicating land nearby, such as plants, insects, and birds; but this should not cause you any problem if you are in 40° or more east, but should if you are to the west where it has not been explored. In these seas are found birds called *centenares* that fly over the surface of the water dodging the waves. They indicate strong winds and at times destructive storms.

Signs of the coast are found at a distance of 70 or 80 leagues, increasing with plants and sea otters, and when nearby, ducks and the colour of very rough water. It is not surprising if fogs are encountered on sighting Cape St. Elias and it will be a good precaution to sound until finding 40 fathoms of water, sandy bottom, and find to the port side a great inlet that forms a horizon between Isla de Santiago and the Cape; but under no pretext will one navigate without it clearing to avoid the risk that the Isla de Carmen that is on the same cape could provide and the Reef of Pamplona, which though it is very small, its rocks jut out more than a league.

At the northwest point of Nootka Entrance there is a reef that looks like a dead whale, to which care will be given, and as soon as it is passed, you will follow the north coast, being careful of the rocks that are seen; but if night falls before arriving at the establishment [of Nootka] and the current carries you, you will anchor in 50 or 60 fathoms.

Finally, in arriving at Nootka, Monterey and the Santa Barbara Channel, you will bear in mind that the fogs are very dense, and that the coast cannot be seen at a distance of one mile, so if you find it that way, the most prudent thing to do would be to tack until it clears.[6]

Other preparations were made for the long northward voyage. A year's supply of foodstuffs was laid aboard with the possibility that the expedition's next reprovisioning might be much later, particularly if they found the northern passage and followed it through to the Atlantic. Some of the ships' gear, more appropriate for operations in tropical and subtropical areas, was left behind in storage in Acapulco, to be reaccessioned at the end of the anticipated itinerary. Spare pieces and parts the use for which could not be foreseen were also left. Some new scientific equipment arrived with Lieutenants José Espinosa and Ciriaco Cevallos, who had overtaken the expedition at Acapulco. As part of their baggage they brought two small Arnold chronometers (numbers 344 and 351) and a simple fixed pendulum which had been made in London, an instrument the explorers soon placed in service. Also, in preparation for the cold weather of a northern campaign, all hands were issued heavy clothing well in advance of actual need.[7]

Specific regulations concerning duties both aboard and ashore had been issued at the outset of the expedition. These had served for the visits of 1789, 1790 and early 1791, simply because all places touched were part of the effective national domain. While on the Northwest Coast, for the first time the expedition would make contact with unpredictable native people, so a series of standing orders governing new conditions was issued. In general, these new instructions called for a doctrine of increased vigilance, of maintaining strength sufficient to meet all possible needs, with elimination of small, widely separated detachments sent on parallel missions. Most of all, they required new anti-personnel measures to prevent sudden attack and possible capture of the corvettes by boarders. To this end, port and starboard watches were instituted, meaning that half the crew was on an alert footing at all times on a twelve-hour rotational basis. The expedition had already had one contact with natives unfamiliar with White society when in December 1789 it made a visit to the Indians of Patagonia. But those Indians were few in number and technologically backward, posing no real threat.

General instructions by reigning Viceroy Revilla Gigedo were lengthy and covered anticipated activity by all ships engaged in northern exploration. The pertinent portion reflects the moderation of that period of Spanish colonial history.

Nothing will be acquired from the Indians against their will; but rather by barter, or by them giving it out of friendship: all must be treated with affability and gentleness, which are the most powerful means to attract them and to firmly establish esteem, so that for those who return to those places with the intention of settling, if such is determined, they will be so treated by the Indians.

For the attentive treatment of the Indians you carry four boxes of beads with 168 strings, with which you can make presents to them, with proper methods of distributing them, since you have to be careful to give more to the principal Indian, who is the superior among them, rather than to the inferior ones.

You must maintain good order among the crew, with which you will take care, both in the navigation as well as when a group must disembark ashore, that there be no lack either of subordination, or of good treatment of the Indians against whom force will never be used, except in the case of it being necessary to defend oneself.[8]

Mindful of the coming northern campaign, preparations were made for possible military action or intervention while in the Pacific Northwest. When only a short distance out of Acapulco, men were assigned for future boat duty. Those chosen were selected from among the most vigorous and strongest. According to one source, those from Galicia and from Andalusia were selected as the best fit for this type of activity. Each boat crew member was to be armed with a gun, two pistols, a cutlass and a knife. One of the most valuable officers, Cayetano Valdés, was selected for command of these special details.[9] The longboats, both the old one and a new one constructed for the *Atrevida* during its stay in San Blas, were altered slightly as a precautionary measure against attack, including the creation of two openings in the stern to permit better ventilation of the small cabin. Practice was afforded the special crews by several unscheduled small boat operations while still at sea.

While on the high seas, but obviously only in favourable weather, officers from one corvette or the other made trips to the sister ship for official purposes on at least four occasions. On one such occasion, the purpose was to solidify plans for the forthcoming operation. Malaspina sent a "spherical map" which depicted all the coast from Bucareli Bay to the eastern side of Kodiak Island. It was based on the earlier works of English captains Cook, Dixon and Nathaniel Portlock; Spanish naval explorers Ignacio Arteaga, Bodega y Quadra and Salvador Fidalgo; and Spanish pilots Gonzalo López de Haro and Estevan Martínez. Since it was felt proper, the Malaspina group preserved the place names already given, with preference for the earliest name bestowed. As a point of reference for comparisons of longitude, it accepted the longitude assigned by Cook to Cape Edgecumbe. In case of separation, which was thought quite possible, the corvettes' point of reunion was set for Port Mulgrave, from which it was thought easiest to reconnoitre the stretch of coast as far as Prince William Sound, utilizing the eastsoutheast winds, which according to travellers in that area were the prevailing ones. It was also decided that once having carried out the principal objective of search for the elusive strait, the party would explore the coast between 50° and 40° north, because concerning that area they had news, though very doubtful, that the English shipowner Richard Cadman Etches had entered Hezeta Strait (now known to be the Columbia River) and discovered an arm of an inland sea. Having finished that inquiry, the

Tlingit helmet, part of a remarkable collection of native artifacts that resulted from the expedition's contact and trade with the Indians at Mulgrave. (Museo de América 13.909)

last stage would be to fix the positions of Cape Mendocino, Monterey Bay, Guadalupe Island and Cape San Lucas, all of which were considered important for Spanish mercantile navigation. This itinerary would bring the corvettes back to Acapulco by the end of 1791.[10]

In the original orders given to Malaspina and Bustamante, and in orders issued by them to their commands, it is clear that Spain was disinterested in commerce with the natives, for the instructions focused on according them such treatment as would win them to allegiance to Spain. It had been determined even before the Malaspina visit that concerning the Northwest Coast Spain would depart from its customary Indian policy of congregation and missionization, although this had been successful in California.

Spain's new control system was: 1) to abandon any attempts at evangelization with the accompanying Franciscans acting only as military chaplains to army and navy personnel; 2) to use gift-giving as a means of attracting and maintaining native friendship and partiality toward Spain, placing it in competition with rival nations; and 3) to establish what promised to be permanent occupation posts of a non-commercial sort. It was a program which had a great command advantage since with few exceptions all participants were military men, not traders. An obvious drawback was expenditure without hope of profit.

In general the expedition's purposes embraced work in many fields, especially in cartography. Many of the officers demonstrated both knowledge and skill in that specialty, with overall responsibility the domain of Felipe Bauzá y Cañas, who from time to time also added to the pictorial record of the expedition by his art work. As chief of charts and maps of the entire expedition, Bauzá played a role of enduring importance.[11]

A regular area of activity, one closely associated with cartography, was astronomy. Hundreds of celestial observations were made, with all officers participating. Most of these sun, moon and star shots were done while in port. A special tent for these observations and for other experiments was set up upon arrival at any point of visitation. In more established areas, the commanding officers arranged with local authorities who provided some unimpeded location to serve such purposes.[12] Astronomical observations were of particular importance in efforts to determine accurate longitude, since latitude was not a problem, nor had it been for centuries. The Malaspina expedition had the latest equipment that Europe had to offer and this was in the hands of skilled observers, to the end that positions established were still considered accurate many years later.

Natural science was of fundamental importance to expedition ends. Plants were collected, organized and categorized according to the Linnean system. Although the Chief of Natural History, Colonel Antonio de Pineda, did not accompany the expedition to the Northwest Coast, Malaspina had the services of one of the small civilian contingent, the Bohemian-born natural scientist Dr. Tadeo Haenke. A remarkable renaissance man, he was not only responsible for much of the botanical investigation, but also doubled as geologist, zoologist, ethnologist and even musician.[13] In addition to the collections which he supervised for the scientific expedition, it is apparent that he made interesting personal acquisitions.[14] In botanical and zoological efforts, the trained scientists were assisted by some of the enlisted personnel and by local Indians who went into the field to gather specimens in accordance with instructions. Nearly all members of the expedition had some role in its scientific objectives. Collecting zoological specimens, hunting and fishing occupied some free time of

Northern flicker Watercolour by José Cardero. (Museo Naval MS 1725; Higueras 3162, Sotos 361)

the assistants. Some incidental trade with local natives was motivated by the scientists' need for specimens in satisfactory condition for study and/or taxidermy. The latter specialty in the hands of some of the crew was earlier something less than a success. Some specimens gradually took on strange and grotesque shapes as a result of unanticipated settling of the materials with which they had been stuffed by enthusiastic amateurs.

During the Pacific Northwest phase of his expedition, Malaspina had the services of two artist-illustrators. Aboard the *Descubierta* was a recent substitute, a talented Spaniard who had been in Mexico since his youth, Tomás de Suria. His assignment aboard the *Descubierta* resulted from a special request made by Malaspina several months in advance of the expedition's arrival in Mexico. The captain's letter written from Guayaquil to the Viceroy of New Spain, the Second Count of Revilla Gigedo, urgently requested a person expert in drawing and perspective who was available to accompany the corvettes on their proposed northern sortie. The artistic record was greatly enhanced by the good fortune that serving on the *Atrevida* was a former cabin boy who gradually became an expedition artist, José Cardero.

Such on-the-spot artistic representation, particularly important to botany, ethnology and zoology, was in large measure the photography of yesteryear. Native types, local customs, general views and objects of curiosity were captured visually, largely on a demand basis. Frequently what we know from the documentary sources is enhanced by the work of artists who served aboard.

A basic part of advance preparation was to gather such material as would further expedition efforts. To that end, even before leaving Spain in 1789, several officers had been sent to the archives in Seville to copy maps and documents needed for future use. Books had been purchased and substantial information gained therefrom was utilized, verified or rejected. Shipments of mail that reached the expedition from time to time also contained the latest news, useful publications and even nautical instruments. Little published information about the Pacific Northwest had been available, only the works of Cook and Dixon, and reports concerning the activities of Lapérouse. The Malaspina expedition had as crew members at least three mariners who are listed in Spanish records as deserters from that earlier French expedition.[15]

Maintenance of personnel strength was of great importance to the expedition, problems being caused in large measure by the prolonged period of absence from their home port of Cádiz. Of the slightly more than 200 men who signed aboard initially for the round-the-world cruise, very few lasted the entire sixty-two months. By the time they had reached Acapulco in 1791, just two years out of their home port, and were staging for the Northwest Coast sortie, the drop-out figure had reached almost 70 per cent of the original crew. Desertion was the greatest problem, with 93 persons, mostly seamen, in that category. Other causes noted were deaths, either aboard or in the hospital (7), personnel left behind in the hospital, crew members transferred off as disobedient or manifesting other irregularities (17) and persons dismissed for habitual accidents (16).[16]

Replacements had to be recruited, and although we know nothing of the specific terms of enlistment of such persons who from time to time presented themselves, it could easily be assumed that these new crew members were not as competent as those from whom Malaspina and Bustamante had been able to draw when in the beginning they had a free hand.[17]

Maritime expertise was a commodity of the marketplace, available to the best bidder from the earliest days of the age of exploration. The farther you were from home, the less likely that those available would be ideally suited for their positions. There seems to have been no great problem in accepting personnel who were not Spanish nationals, and from the available sources, such as the guard books and the communion lists, it is estimated that as many as 20 per cent of the combined crews were non-Spanish, a considerable number of whom were not even able to communicate in that language. There was nothing new about the use of mercenaries. Even at the highest levels such as Columbus, Cabot, Verrazano, Magellan, Cermeño, Hudson and Bering, foreign nationals were customarily employed. At lower levels it was perhaps even more common. Rather than using the lesser skills of their own nationals, and certainly in the absence of satisfactory personnel, use of non-Spaniards was the most logical solution. Immediately prior to departure for the Pacific Northwest, the depleted ranks of the corvettes were replenished in part by some Filipino mariners who were in Acapulco as a result of the galleon trade with Manila.

Some important members of the Malaspina expedition did not participate in the northern voyage of 1791. Colonel Pineda, Chief of Natural History, spent his time in excursions to various parts of Mexico from Mexico City, where he made his headquarters. Botanist Luis Née, a civilian member of the expedition, did likewise. Dionisio Alcalá Galiano, who later played an important role in the Pacific Northwest as senior commander of the 1792 subexpedition, had remained in Mexico in 1791 as head of a small commission consisting of fellow officers Manuel Novales, Arcadio Pineda (brother of the chief of natural history) and Martín Olavide to coordinate reports of previous activity in advancing the study of geography of New Spain, to which end time was spent in collecting materials from the viceregal archives in the capital.

It was not required that all information gathered be original within the Malaspina group, since it had access to several other sources beyond archival documents. Local informants possessed intimate knowledge, and whether giving information for the first time or making use of the fruits of their own inquiries, these persons added substantially and usually precisely to Malaspina's resources. Upon some of these sources reports were written, or later secondary studies by the explorers were based. Even local natives were used as informants, not only concerning their own culture, which might be expected, but also on other areas of interest to the scientists.

The efficiency of work of the naval explorers is a source of admiration which at the same time might be a source of error. In a brief period of ten days spent at Yakutat and another two weeks at Santa Cruz de Nutka, they gathered a considerable record. It is obvious that little time was lost when in port, making every hour count. Probably the greatest problem was that of allocation of time to different aspects of work, particularly if armed escorts were needed for protection. Different individuals and groups had already developed their expertise, a fact conducive to such efficiency as resulted. Viewed in retrospect, we always wish for more on some subjects and less repetition between sources, and for this we would willingly forego so much detail on things such as celestial observations. On the other hand, accounts such as those worked up by the scientific expedition members are generally superior to other sources. As might logically be anticipated, many of the personnel assigned to the Malaspina expedition were aboard to carry out the-day-to day operation of the corvettes at sea or in port. Not only were most of the crew of each corvette dedicated to some routine duty, but also a large area of cargo space was needed for non-technical operation. This included stowage of foodstuffs, naval stores, clothing and other gear. Except for the projected length of the voyage, these factors differed little from traditional naval operations. In armament the *Descubierta* and *Atrevida* were less well equipped than standard corvettes since the expectation of offensive armed warfare was almost nil, while the need for defensive action was restricted to the possibility of having to repel militarily unsophisticated native boarders. This fact reduced the area of munitions storage and the weight of guns, thereby freeing space to be utilized for scientific purposes.

Some officers and most enlisted men were primarily engaged in shipboard routine. Few, if any, officers escaped completely from the regular duties of commissioned officers, no matter how important their scientific functions might be. All regular officers and midshipmen stood duty watches in port and deck watches while underway. Some scientific expeditions of the period with similar objectives to the Malaspina group had two independent sets of officers, with maritime management of the ships assigned to regular naval officers while the scientific officers were hardly more than passengers while at sea. But Malaspina's group made use of almost all key personnel in both capacities, beginning with Malaspina and Bustamante. One of the physicians, Dr. Pedro María González, also helped with natural science, being knocked off some medical routine which was shifted to his colleague.[18] One of the pursers spent long hours as a copyist putting documents in final form. Only four men can be identified as doing only specialized work – a botanist, a natural scientist and two artists, one on each ship. Even the artists did both general and technical illustrations. Cardero, the unofficial artist, did many things – cabin boy, scribe, pilot and journalist.

Logistics consumed considerable time in coordination, procurement, proper stowage and eventual disbursement. When in major ports such as Acapulco, local suppliers were available, but there were never any docking facilities to make on-loading easy. On all occasions lighterage was necessary, whether provided locally or carried out by the corvettes' crews and small boats. When in areas devoid of port facilities such as Port Mulgrave or of limited facilities such as Nootka and Monterey, loading was accomplished by the men and equipment of the *Descubierta* and *Atrevida*. The ships' longboats or launches were utilized for heavy work, while raft-like conveyances (*bombos*) were used for some other tasks.

Provisioning

Of essential logistic jobs, the most important were obtaining food and potable water. Large quantities of staple foods, such as hardtack, rice, beans, chocolate, chickpeas and bacon, were supplemented by more perishable items. In port, when available as in Monterey, green vegetables, fruit, milk, fresh meat and other local produce supplemented the mariners' diet, a daily fare that when at sea was ample in quantity but monotonous.

Unlike many extended cruises, the Malaspina expedition, because of the scientific nature of its primary mission, spent considerably more time in port than at sea, thus making food supply a problem of lesser magnitude. This division between time at sea and time in port reduced the incidence of dietary deficiency disease. Evidence of poor nutrition was not totally lacking, but it was not particularly attributable to being at sea. Empirical observations were made on dietary matters, particularly by Dr. González of the Corvette *Atrevida*, who after completion of the expedition wrote and published a lengthy treatise on illnesses at sea.[19] Much of the material was taken from his experiences between 1789 and 1795. From this published source we learn with some precision of the rations issued under normal circumstances. For each person aboard, biscuit or hardtack was set at 560 grams a day, while legumes were 940 grams per week. Water was rationed at four litres a day and wine at a half-litre daily. Cheese, 155 grams, replaced meat on Fridays, and 720 grams of bacon or salted meat were set aside weekly. The basic diet also included rations of vinegar, olive oil, garlic and salt. Special efforts were made to maintain fresh supplies for the longest possible time. To this end, live animals such as chickens, calves, goats and pigs were set aboard as deck cargo assigned to special pens. At Monterey, four young steers were taken aboard. Protein was augmented by acquisition of eggs and by fishing or trading for fish, particularly when on the Northwest Coast an exquisite salmon could be had for as little as a button. Such trade, setting aside twentieth-century concepts of value, was ideal, each trade partner obtaining something of considerable value to himself in exchange for something that was nearly valueless to him because of its abundance and ease of acquisition.

Fish, when obtained in large quantities, were substituted in the daily ration aboard ship for the equivalent amount of bacon. Since the daily ration of bacon was from two to four ounces (except for Fridays, when none was given), a few large salmon would have a dietary impact. Fish caught also served as specimens for dissection, classification and illustration. Somewhat surprisingly, the Pacific Northwest phase of Malaspina's voyage produced little by way of ichthyological illustration despite the presence of two competent artists and a richness of available fish.

Water was resupplied as circumstances permitted, the need being almost never completely filled. Casks were stowed below deck with utmost care to prevent leakage and unnecessary movement. Notwithstanding the best efforts, water sometimes went bad, and there was always concern whether any current source was better or worse than the water already aboard. The ideal situation was a plentiful spring of clear fresh water found near the shore to reduce the labour in handling the casks, particularly after they were treated[20] and filled. The water detail was of such importance that an officer was assigned and the number of barrels obtained was entered into the Guard Book as an event of the day. Part of the routine involved inspection of casks to determine their condition and to repair any that were damaged.

The *Descubierta* and *Atrevida* were also capable of making fresh water when at sea, since each had evaporators with an iron firebox, providing a moderate distilling capacity. The problem of making water at sea was linked with the availability of fuel to heat the water. When water was short, fuel was almost always also in low supply.

A regular job while in port was gathering firewood for stowage aboard, since cooking was done over wood stoves. Fuel gathering details were frequently commingled with the water detail. Fallen timber was best since it was dry and easier to manage. On the Northwest Coast there was no shortage of trees and thus the wood detail met with easy success. There is no evidence that obtaining of any commodity, whether water, wood or ballast, in such limited quantities as taken by Malaspina's group, was resented by the local Indians as an unwarranted appropriation of tribal property, though such had apparently been the case in 1775 with a Spanish group that had gone ashore from the Hezeta expedition while along the Washington coast near Point Grenville. That early incident led to disaster.[21]

Ballast, a constant requirement of seagoing vessels of that period, was another logistic need. Such cargo, carried for its weight alone and usually in the form of stones or sacks of sand, was for stabilizing the sailing condition of ships. Loading of ballast required a satisfactory, easily handled source to make the effort worthwhile, one located very close to the shore to reduce what at best was tedious work. Subsequent disposal of ballast was frequently done at sea with the result that resupply was needed from time to time.

Salt for use in cooking and as a preservative was not available at all locations. Its acquisition was of sufficient importance to be precisely entered into the Guard Book when, after the visit to the Northwest Coast, a generous supply was taken from salt beds close to the mouth of the Salinas River near Monterey in California.

On Board Ship

In an era when such was not common, Malaspina was greatly interested in the cleanliness of both men and vessels under his command. While en route to Mulgrave, he ordered the vessel cleaned, scrubbed and swept so as to maintain conditions of sanitation sufficient to prevent any contagious disease. On at least four occasions, for purposes of ventilation, he ordered the crew to take out their clothing and other luggage from between decks and put them on top of the boats. Suria's journal entry records that this was done "all with favourable results, very much to the satisfaction of our commander who gives the orders and to the doctor and his assistant, Don Tadeo [Haenke], who are very diligent in preventing any unfortunate casualty among our crew."[22] Such attention to cleanliness was not sufficient to rid the vessels of the inevitable swarm of cockroaches. Artist Suria complained about this inconvenience at the same time that he indicated in his journal that he was greatly cramped for space. "I will only say that stretched in my bed my feet were against the side of the ship and my head against the bulkhead, which is what they call the timbers that enclose the cabin. From my breast to the deck, which was my roof, the distance is only three inches. This confined position does not allow me to move in my bed and I am forced to make for myself a roll of cloth to cover my head, although this suffocates me, but this is a lesser evil than being attacked by thousands of cockroaches, which are such a great pest that you see some individuals with sores on their foreheads and bites on their fingers."[23] If such crowded conditions obtained in officer's country, where the civilian artist was billeted, it is unsettling to imagine what those who sailed before the mast as enlisted personnel must have experienced.

A duty of the ship's doctor was to test the air periodically in various parts of the vessel by use of an eudiometer. This device invented by Felix Fontana, an Italian physiologist, measured the wholesomeness of air in terms of the quantity of good air in a specific sample, the result being expressed as a percentage. On 19 May, Dr. Francisco Flores started measuring from the hold up "in order to make useful regulations to secure the conservation of the health of our crew." On the following day in the boatswain's locker, the eudiometer registered 60 parts of good air, whereas the storeroom showed 57 per cent of pure air, the lower figure being attributed by Dr. Flores to the presence of corruptible materials, the fermentation of which fouled the air. Similar experiments were performed on atmospheric air and the air between decks, with the finding being that the air between

Explicacion de las Reparticiones del Buque.

A Camara de Estudio: contiene una pequeña Biblioteca de Mesitas y una Chimenea Ynglesa. En el Imperio de el Comandante es el con el Escribir

B Camara de los Ynstrumentos Astronomicos, Meteorologicos y Relox marino

C Cinco Camaras para otros Sres. Plana mayor, igual numero á Estrivor: El Espacio comprehendido entre las Camaras ocupa toda banda, forma una Camara con una altura etcetera de siete pies y ocho Pesetas

D Escotillon p.ª bajar á los Pañoles á Pan

E Repostería comunica por una mesita fuera con la Camara p.ª servir con comodidad: está en el medio de Estrivor con Cara Ynglesa

F Dos ... etcetera

G Lugar abitable p.ª la Tropa y p.ª la Marinería: El Ganado está colocado á el medio entre la Escotilla y Cubertura mayor

H Cubertura mayor: Viene del Escrivador con un Recorro á popa, etcetera entre la Bomba y el Palo mayor

Y El Gran Escala contra ...

K Comunicacion del Pañolero con el Sollado

L Santa Barbara contra Chillar p.ª Pañol Lalanquera y metralla, al cargo del Piloto, el del Herrero, Varios Utencilios y Escaparates

M Un Camarote con dos Caras por cada lado.

N Pañoles grandes á Bavor y Estrivor para Vestuario, efectos de Cambio, Alhas, Repuesto de Estmeras y algunos ...

O Pañol de Velas

P Sitio para los Cables ...

Q Bodega con viveres, Aguada, Leña y Agua ...

R Custodia de Caras y Equipages. El Cerrajero á Estrivor es para el Rancho de la Camara.

S Un Pañol p.ª Cargo del Carp.º Calafate, Carpinero, Escrisales, etcetera

T Escotilla de Proa: El es la Escotilla á Estrivor Cara de Estrivor p.ª y Utencilio algunos útiles del Naturalista

V Despensa conteniendo lo necesario p.ª la Subministracion Diaria de Racion: A Estrivor un Pañol Grande del Contramaestre

X Pañol p.ª Betunes, Estmeria, Carbon.

Z Pañucho para efectos del Constructor.

Ꝺ Pañol de Polvora p.ª 50 quintales.

Dotacion de las Corbetas

Descubierta		Atrevida	
Comand.te de la Exp.n Cap.n de Navio	D. Alessandro Malaspina 1	Comand.te Cap.n de Fragata	D. Jose Bustamante y Guerra 1
Cap.n de Fragata	D. Cayetano Valdez 1		D. Ant.º Tova y Arredondo 1
	D. Manuel de Novales		D. Dionisio Galiano
	D. Jose Fontanar Sous		D. Juan Gut. de la Concha
	D. Jose Maria de Sousa 6		D. Josef Robredo 6
	D. Juan Bernaci y ...		D. Ciriaco Cevallos
	D. Secundino Salamanca		D. Fernando de Clavijo
Contador	D. Rafael Pedroza Rey 1	Contador	D. Manuel Ezquerra 1
Capellan	D. Josef de Mesa 1	Capellan	D. Juan de Paula Arino 1
Cirujano	D. Pedro Maria Gonzalez 1	Cirujano	D. Jose Maria Gonzalez 1
Piloto Marina	D. Pedro Maria Pineda 1	Pilotos	D. Isidro Murphy 1
Primer Piloto	D. Felipe Bauza 1	2.º Piloto	D. Juan Diaz Maqueda 1
Pilotines	2	Pilotines	2
Contram.e	1	Contram.e	1
Guardian 1.º	2	Guardian 1.º	2
Sangrador	1	Sangrador	1
Carpinteros	3	Carpinteros	3
Calafates	3	Calafates	3
Herrero	1	Herrero	1
Buzo	1	Buzo	1
Cocin. de Equip.e	2	Cocin. de Equip.e	2
Pañolero	1	Pañolero	1
Esperanzas	1	Esperanzas	1
Artilleros	35	Artilleros	35
Grumetes	10	Grumetes	10
Sarg. de Art.ª	1	Sarg. de Art.ª	1
Cabos de Art.ª	2	Cabos de Art.ª	2
Soldados	12	Soldados	12
Condestable	1	Condestable	1
Sarg.to de Brig.da	3	Sarg.to de Brig.da	3

Noticia de los Instrumentos Mathematicos Geodesicos y Fisicos contenidos en ambas Corbetas.

Descubierta	Atrevida
Relox de Berthoud n.º 10	Relox de Berthoud n.º 10
Cronometro de Arnold n.º 72	Cronometro de Arnold n.º 71
Cronometro de Arnold n.º 61	Relox de Jalsinguera n.º 105 propio del Comand.te
Un Quadrante Astronomico de Ramsden y 20 pulg.s de Radio	Un Inas Astronom.º de ... en dos pies de Radio
Un Relox de Segund.s de Jalsinguera	Un Relox de Segund.s de Jalsinguera
Quatro Anteojos Astronomicos	tres anteojos astronomicos
Un aguja de Inclinac.n de Naime	Una aguja de Inclinac.n de Naime
Dos agujas acimutales de Maime	Dos agujas acimutales de Maime y Knight
y Knight	Dos Teodolites
Dos Teodolites	Un Barometro marino de Na...
Un Pendulo Astronomico	...
Un Barometro de Naime	Uno id. de Magallanes
Uno id. de Magallanes	
Dos Barometros de etcetera...	Nota
Una camara optica	No habimos llegado á tpo las com...
Doce tubos Capilares p.ª el mismo uso	... faltan Varios instrumentos de fisica y
Un anteojo grande terrestre	Chimica.
Quatro chicos p.ª expedicion de tierra	
Uno de noche	Van
Un nivel de agua p.ª los princip.s	...
de Carcell	...
Un barometro p.ª estimar el term... pesa el agua á una prefundid.d qualquiera.	
Un Relox p.ª Carrera	
Dos peramitros con etcetera	
Un Grande Chimico	
Una Coleccion de Chimica para...	

decks was more healthful than that of the atmosphere "to the extent of five parts." The doctor opined that this was on account of nearness of the cook stove in the galley which purified the air.[24]

While headed north, circumstances permitted an occasional visit while at sea, one of which resulted from an unanticipated event of 22 May aboard the *Atrevida*, while the corvettes were still far from their destination. It was a problem that threatened the explorers with a serious setback.

In the little scientific world of the corvettes an occurrence of importance took place. Chronometer number 10, manufactured by Berthod, was found stopped, but not for lack of winding; and although it was given several horizontal shakes, with the same precaution as had been taken in similar cases, it was not possible to put it into motion. Word was passed to Don Alejandro Malaspina, and shortly thereafter he came aboard to inform himself in detail of the measures taken and to bring with him the instructions for its operation as written by the manufacturer. This marvelous instrument which when operated by able hands had such a part in the astonishing sailing directions of the combined squadron, had maintained an almost perfect synchronism ever since Cádiz, and its loss would have been irreplaceable if we did not have five other longitude chronometers, all by Arnold, and most of them of the highest reliability. In the afternoon, and after having read the instructions of the manufacturer, they again repeated the experiments done at midday, and thinking it proper, the receptacle in which the chronometer was held was heated until the thermometer reached 22 degrees. All was useless and fearing risks that the instrument might suffer from the continual rolling of the ship, we ceased for the time being the effort of putting it into motion.[25]

On 27 May, Malaspina and José Espinosa tried again. Espinosa was particularly familiar with chronometer number 10 since he had used it for a long time as a member of the commission to draw up the

Cutaway drawing of the identical corvettes, the Descubierta *and the* Atrevida, *with a manifest indicating the disposition of provisions and crew. Special stowage arrangements are indicated for scientific equipment, as well as a working area in the stern for the use of the scientists. (Museo de América 2.340; Palau 1, Sotos 788)*

Chronometers such as this one, #71, made by John Arnold in London, probably in 1787 or 1788, and acquired for Malaspina's expedition, were used to determine longitude during a voyage. (Museo Naval I-1276; Higueras 3242)

Hydrographic Atlas of Spain. Between them, they had no success. The chronometer was opened and the body of the instrument examined with great care to make certain that there was no small break or dislocation of pieces, but try as they might, it was to no avail and resulted in postponement of further work on the chronometer,[26] leaving it stopped rather than taking it apart. The malfunction was ascribed to the thickness of the lubricating oil, combined with some cold that caused condensation.[27]

While at sea en route to Mulgrave, military drill was held almost on a daily basis. This was supplemented by regular gunnery practice. Other measures were taken to maintain rigorous discipline, particularly in the use of firearms, the "handling of which would be essentially needed by the sailors who would man the launches," such men having been selected to "combine true valour with peaceful conduct and who without ceasing to be of usefulness when it might be necessary, would neither foster arguments with the natives nor give rise to such."[28]

Good weather on the passage north was occasionally punctuated by heavy rainstorms, but none which greatly impeded the plan of navigation. From 15 June on, the corvettes began to enjoy even more favourable weather with few calms or adverse winds from the northwest and the north. On 17 June, when in almost 48° north, signs of the nearness of the coast were first seen in the form of *porras*, an easily recognizable seaweed that looked like a blackjack. Ships bound from Manila for over two centuries welcomed its appearance as a sign of being within 220 leagues of the coast, an omen announcing the end of their difficult trans-Pacific crossing. At the same time the Malaspina group saw whale calves and aquatic birds, even more propitious signs of their nearness to land.

Upon sighting the northwest coast on 23 June, expedition officers took bearings on the land. The first area recognized was Cape Engaño, which Captain Cook had called Cape Edgecumbe, and the nearby mountain of the same name on Kruzof Island. When the entire coast came into view, Suria described it as a "very broken and mountainous land, with some peaks and points very sharp and unequal, the summits of which were covered with snow, just like the mountain at the cape."[29] Both the geographer, Felipe Bauzá y Cañas, and First Pilot Juan Maqueda took bearings and determined correctly that the mountain was in 57°. "From here the coast begins to turn towards the west forming an extensive horseshoe which ends in Bering's Strait, where the last part of America ends, and Asia then continues."[30] Both Bauzá and Suria drew a view of the cape. The longitude of Cape Engaño was calculated with great exactness, which compared with that of Cook gave a difference of 13' to the east, while noting at the same time two strange things: that the movement of all of the chronometers was advanced, and that all of the eastern distances, while agreeing with each other, varied one degree from the western ones, which were also uniform.[31]

The *Descubierta* and *Atrevida* next stood off from the coast in an effort to gain higher latitude, which made it impossible to determine at that time the true position of the ports of Guadalupe and Remedios which Bodega had visited in 1775. A series of mound-shaped islands hid from them any openings at a time when such were being sought, but it did not stop them from seeing Captain Cook's Monte de la Cruz, from which follows the cordillera that ends at Mount Fairweather, "which even at this so favourable time is covered with snow even along its slopes."[32]

On 24 June, very high mountains were seen in the distance, all

One of two quadrants, made by Jesse Ramsden in London and purchased for the expedition. They were set up on shore to ensure accurate celestial observations. (Museo Naval I-778; Higueras 3239)

covered with snow. The geographer took bearings on them and drew a view, as did Suria. By 25 June, the corvettes had doubled Cape Fairweather, whereupon the artist wrote:

A chain of mountains with Mount Buen Tiempo [Fairweather], the highest and greatest, hangs over the sea. It causes the greatest wonder and admiration to see them all covered with the purest snow from the foot to the summit, and the eyes do not tire of looking at them. I placed myself on the poop in order to make a sketch of them, but the frigid air which came off them made me stop very soon as I could not stand it. I went down to the quarter gallery on the port side and there without being so cold I drew a view, a great part of which the geographer adopted, adding it to the rest of the collection. Today we are in 58° 40'.[33]

The next day another range was sighted, though the sky was quite cloudy. This area was more covered with trees, but various streaks of snow on the side presented a pleasing view. One wide streak ran down from the summit to the beach in a "wriggly" manner – a glacier. Between the geographer and Suria, a good view of the scene was made.[34]

Under advantageous sailing conditions, the corvettes ran the coast seeking any indications of the long-sought strait. Sailing about a league distant from the islands that form the port of Mulgrave and having gone some distance on that course, the explorers spotted an inlet "the appearances of which had the most exact conformity with those seen by [Lorenzo] Ferrer Maldonado" over two centuries earlier.[35] The view that spread before them was varied. To the port side the coast continued with a range of mountains, "very steep and rough, and black from the foot half way up. This, with the contrast of the snow on the summits and some gorges above, makes a beautiful sight, although wild and uncommon."

On the starboard side and in front of the coast are many islands and low
rocks, all densely forested with pine trees. From now on the cold began to
bother us a great deal, so much so that we could hardly stand it, as there
was so much snow on all sides and the fog was so thick that we could
scarcely see the Atrevida, although she was quite close to us. When we
were in the middle of this first small bay, the geographer [Bauzá] saw an
opening which divided the range of mountains, forming a small strait.
Within, a small inlet presented itself to our view. Great was the joy of the
commander and of all the officers because they believed, and with some
foundation, that this might be the so much desired and sought-for strait,
which would form a passage from the North Sea of Europe and which
has cost so much trouble to all the nations in various expeditions which
they have made for simply this end, and for the discovery of which a great
reward has been offered.[36]

First Contact: Port Mulgrave

Much attention was given to reconnaissance of the opening, this possible entrance to the fabled Northwest Passage, but from where the vessels were, it was not possible to see the extent or the nature of its end. "Transported with joy," wrote Suria "our commander steered towards the opening, sounding at each instant, but when near it, forty fathoms were found, and he determined to anchor in the port of Mulgrave, discovered in the year 1787 by Dixon, and from there with the boats of the two corvettes, which are [properly] equipped, to reconnoitre this entrance and a great portion of the coast which is to be explored before reaching the Port of Prince William, discovered by Captain Cook."[1] It was felt best to attempt such an inspection in the ships' boats while the corvettes held a stationary position inside the port that they knew existed just beyond a projecting point of land.

When they were within a league of the desired port, the corvettes were intercepted by two native canoes, the occupants of which greeted the strangers with music and other signs of peace. A chief came aboard and apparently sought hostages, with some urgency, a request which was summarily denied by the arriving Spaniards. In a brief while, more significant visitors approached in a two-man kayak. Of the two new arrivals, "one was a venerable old man who came aboard, strode across the quarterdeck with an affected timidity, launched into a long discourse full of enthusiasm, shifting his voice from the sky, to the sea, to us and to his own people, from which we learned that he [Ankau] was the principal chief of the natives." He also confirmed this and indicated that the younger man who accompanied him, whom the Spaniards at first thought was the more important, was actually his son. To demonstrate this, he held his arms in the position of holding a child, moving them as is done for lulling a baby. Tova's journal continues the story:

The chief demonstrated great desire that we anchor near his village in which he had his objects of interest; he was most expert in sign language and answered well many of our questions, some of which concerned the nature of the opening seen that morning; but not understanding and suspecting that we thought of anchoring over in that direction, he told us 'that its inhabitants were very fierce and would kill us unmercifully,' whereas toward the Port of Mulgrave we would find means to satisfy our needs and even our passions, explaining this last point by unmistakable signs.[2]

A fresh breeze continued all day long, preventing entry into the port and forcing the corvettes to tack continually. An afternoon rain did not deter the natives, who in their canoes had surrounded the incoming vessels, nor did it stop some available women from remaining on the beach until 7 P.M. Meanwhile the corvettes, taking advantage of the tide, were able to pass the point where the scientific observatory would later be set up and to head for the anchorage. The security measures already established by the Spaniards led Malaspina to make signs to the Indians who had come aboard the corvettes that they should go ashore. Trade of beads for sea otter skins would be better consummated there. The natives understood the signal, but they did not stop following during the entire afternoon,

always singing songs which, although harsh on account of the pronunciation, were not very disagreeable. The King or chief went about directing his canoes in one made of skin, shaped like a weaver's shuttle with a deck of the same material in which there were two perfectly round holes by which they enter and leave, and which reach to their waist, where they tie them. In these canoes [kayaks] they pass from one island to the other, and when there are bad storms and heavy seas, they get inside them and leave them to the force of the waves, and are very secure as water does not enter anywhere.[3]

By 7:30 P.M., the *Descubierta* and *Atrevida* were anchored in ten fathoms of water, about a pistol shot from the beach and opposite the Tlingit village of Chief Ankau. Subsequently, a kedge anchor and a cable were added in an effort to hold their positions. This initial anchorage brought forth from Suria the following comment: "This bay is very beautiful, all surrounded with various rocky islands, covered by big pine forests which present a beautiful view. I do not know its size, but from what can be seen, it seems to me it might be a little more or less than six leagues in circumference."[4]

The local natives were astounded and watched in silence, "and perhaps not without some fear," the Spanish activity of lowering the small boats into the water, particularly in the case of the launches. As night approached, the visitors by using signs said good night to the natives and looked forward to some rest from their difficult time in taking the vessels into the harbour.

The visitors knew in advance that 'uncivilized', armed Indians, as those on the Northwest Coast were thought to be, could pose a security threat, one that required increased vigilance. Concerning the natives of Mulgrave, up to this point, even while still aboard ship, the Spaniards had been able to "form some idea of their character and propensities," so the crews of the *Descubierta* and *Atrevida* already exercised the greatest caution in dealing with them, not allowing any Indians to come aboard nor to begin to carry out their eagerly-sought exchanges "except for a few of little importance which the sailors carried out furtively."[5]

Security instructions issued to his officers by Malaspina at the time of arrival at Mulgrave called for unusually tight control over expedition activities.

In the port where we now find ourselves and which we continue to call by the name Port Mulgrave, we must predetermine as essential the two objectives of providing ourselves with ballast, water and firewood and of maintaining by our choice a peaceful contact with the natives [without which] it seems that attainment of the astronomical observations and the examination of the oscillations of the pendulum that has been proposed to me will be quite difficult. The following precautions directed toward the greatest uniformity in our dealings will make evident aboard both vessels the orders that I have set forth for that purpose.

1st. As soon as the environs of the port are explored and the place is determined where we are to gather our supply of ballast, water and wood, the personnel of the two corvettes assigned to the work will form a single unit; that is, they will be at the orders of a single officer and guarded by a single squad of soldiers. The clear instructions for the officer thus assigned will then extend specifically for the purpose of clearing up this matter with the greatest pointedness.

2nd. Without occasioning any violence or displeasing the natives, it will be attempted to have trading done ashore rather than aboard, and that a convenient place be set apart, and that complete order be established and with an officer present and a small squad. All the formality possible will be given to this market so that there be no quarrels nor deceit and so that trading may be carried out with full awareness.

3rd. To anyone who without the express permission of the commanding officer or the officer in charge, and to anyone who goes further than the prescribed limits, either at the place of taking water and wood or at the place of the observatory, and of trading will be severely punished on pain of six months in chains or shackles if he be a sailor or soldier, and a year of detention if he be of the other subaltern classes. In case anyone gets into a quarrel which leads to or comes close to hostilities, either among our people or among the natives, he will be severely punished according to the importance of the offense, under the supposition that no person should separate from the environs of the officer in command of the squad, not even after he may have been robbed. Nor will he cease to be a culprit even if he were not the first offender, if he does not come

immediately to present his complaints to the officer without taking other measures himself.

4th. The artillery will be loaded with a single cartridge; there will be some firearms fully ready for any purpose. Those forming the guard as sentinels will not leave the deck and this guard shall consist of three, two from the troop and one from the seamen or vice versa; there will be all possible vigilance, and from eight P.M. on, they will pass the word between those on each corvette and with those ashore, if there be any.

5th. If the daily acquisition of fish and plants can be systematized in quantity and uniform exchange, these useful items will be substituted on both ships for part of the daily allowance, especially that of bacon.

6th. No boat can go off for the purpose of fishing (which for the time being will be suspended) without an officer and some fire arms. It is ordered on this occasion not to use them except in the greatest necessity and with the least harm; and as for hunting, it will be best that those who are not very expert do not do so, in order not to reduce the fear of their havoc.

7th. During the day the principal objectives of the officers will be directed toward a most personal knowledge of the language of the natives, and concerning the language they will pay particular attention to those words that have the most direct connection with the objectives of good relations; and finally, they will not use any word whatsoever the meaning of which is not understood whenever the conversation tends toward an argument or to an offense on their part.

8th. The naval officers are to be charged that they try not to mix with the troop or crew, even in trading. These are the precautions that are to be followed at present, and the exact fulfillment of which is entrusted especially to the officers of both corvettes.[6]

The following morning, 28 June, the Spaniards assessed their position and recognized that they were in a pleasant environment. Malaspina felt that, despite the rainy and overcast conditions, everything pointed to a peaceful climate. Their anchoring ground was in 12 fathoms, mud bottom, in a port that "might have better been called a dock." It was close to the beach and the native Indians in considerable numbers were so near at hand that, without misgivings or bother, a study could be made of their customs. Furthermore, water, wood, ballast, fish and edible plants, all the necessary things, were so accessible that taking them aboard could not even be considered any trouble.

Early in the morning the commanding officers went ashore, along with some of the officers, soldiers and marines, to establish friendly relations with the local Indians. The Tlingits, who interspersed music with much of their activities, made the sign of peace and burst into song so loud that the native voices could be heard from on board the corvettes.

One of the first activities, one assisted by Chief Ankau, was to find a place to take water. This was done after a few useless efforts, the spot being a small inlet opposite the anchoring ground and to the east.[7] Even this was not fully satisfactory since the Spaniards, with all the native help and their own activities, could only find a spring of still water, the taste of which savoured of the roots through which it had passed. The site was chosen with the hope of improving it by making the water run. Before returning aboard, the Spaniards prodigiously rewarded for their small service the Indian man and three women who lived in two huts near the spring, whom they understood were either husband and wives, or all related.[8]

Early during the first complete day in port, the explorers found their vessels surrounded by many Indians, both men and women, attracted by the novelty of the newcomers and by a desire to trade objects that they had made. In the acquisition of such items the sailors showed great curiosity. At first the Indians climbed up on the quarterdeck, but later they were ordered to lay below to the launch in order to prevent robberies and other disorders, while still allowing them to propose their exchanges. One Indian had made off with a pennant, which he returned with great serenity immediately upon being reprimanded; he did not return an iron padlock, but rather had the impertinence of showing to Ensign Jacobo Murphy, officer of the day, his dagger ("an arm of common use among them"), as if demonstrating his determination to defend the stolen object come what may. The Spaniards thought that "It would have been very easy to punish the audacity of this insolent man if we had not been resolved to avoid, as much as possible, any quarrel." The Mulgrave chief came aboard a little later, and when informed of the robbery, he harangued the natives and the padlock which was already ashore was returned aboard in a few minutes. This incident did not interrupt trade because, according to Lieutenant Commander Tova, "the anxiousness with which our people bought the vilest objects for the sole reason of it having belonged to the natives, opened every minute a new line of trade."[9]

In addition to fish, the Tlingits brought their fishing gear, their domestic items, their arms and other objects of their own manufacture, all of which they exchanged for old clothing, nails, buttons and other similar articles at a fair price for both parties. The Spaniards noted that when the Tlingits agreed upon an exchange, they all sang. Such singing was an integral part not only of trade, but also of many other activities, so the air was filled with music during the visit of the foreigners. During the afternoon of the same day, 28 June, Chief Ankau, who had been aboard the *Atrevida* all morning, went over to the *Descubierta*. There Suria drew the native leader's likeness with considerable fidelity; on being shown his portrait, the chief was so pleased that

Ankau, chief of the Mulgrave Tlingit. Ink and wash drawing by Tomás de Suria. (Suria Diary, Bienicke Library, Yale University; Sotos, 580)

he vehemently insisted that he be drawn wearing a helmet which in a bloody combat he had taken from an enemy leader.[10]

In dealing with the natives, Malaspina found them in their stratagems of trade to be as previously described by the English Captain Dixon. The would-be traders brought whatever they intended to exchange completely covered and appeared to be completely indifferent to the business. After up to an hour or more, during which time they remained quiet in spite of there being within view many objects that were offered to them, finally, they would take out a part of a pelt, or a bag, or a spoon, or any trinket whatsoever, and attempt to trade it for everything they saw. If they could not pass off their trade object for its quality, they called attention to its size and symmetry. Once the Tlingit traders had agreed to a bargain, they reneged. At last, if among the things they brought there was a really good pelt, they showed it with such mystery, letting it be seen, then withdrawing it, to the point where they aroused in the most indifferent soul a mixture of ire and desire, difficult to explain. There was not noted in the Mulgraves any spirit of competition either in acquisition or sale of items; rather they pooled their interest or consulted among themselves before finalizing a trade. If they consummated a trade, they applauded it with one, two or three unanimous acclamations, in accordance with their idea of the advantage that they had gained.[11]

On 29 June, the observatory tent was taken ashore. The Indians were even more eager for trade and were "very sociable," for in return for clothing buttons, which they hung as pendants from their ears, they traded some rich, fresh salmon, at the rate of a salmon for a button. "We could never satisfy ourselves with it notwithstanding that we ate an abundance of it,"[12] wrote Suria on the visitors' liking for this fish.

Chief Ankau, who came alongside with his two sons, the eldest a very ferocious and large Indian, asked by signs to be allowed to come aboard. The captain permitted this and the chief was entertained in the captain's cabin. "There was much to wonder at about these three men," wrote Suria. "The chief was an old, venerable and ferocious looking man with a very long grey beard, in a pyramidal form, his hair flaccid and loose on his shoulders. False hair over it in various locks, without any order or arrangement, made him look like a monster."[13] Suria drew a likeness on the spot. A large "lion" skin, probably a brown bear pelt, was used as a cape, gathered in at the waist and leaving entirely bare his "breast, arms, thighs and endowments, all very muscular and strong." This gave to Ankau a somewhat majestic air, "which he manifested by speaking but little, measuredly, and with a sound which at times seemed to be the bellow of a bull. At other times it was softer and in speaking to his sons it was sweeter than in conversation." The elder of the two sons was nearly two metres tall, and equally stout and muscular. "He had his hair loose which, on account of its thickness, seemed like a horse's mane. It was very black like that of his beard. He was dressed in a very hairy black bear skin, also in the form of a cloak, which he fastened with some ornament, leaving bare at times all his nakedness, and passing to and fro over the quarterdeck, very proud and straight, his demeanour full of ire, arrogant and condescending."

The visiting Tlingit began to explain to the Spaniards by signs that other ships had been there and that they had seen them. These, the visitors inferred, were those of Dixon from 1787. With very strange gestures and postures, they also explained about some battle, an action which showed the Spaniards that the Tlingits were very warlike. "What we could draw from all their signs was that a short time before, they had fought some other chief who had killed the son of their chief. They showed us his helmet, which was of a [decorative] figure, and an extraordinary construction of wood, copper, and of straw cloth, and with a mask in front which appeared to be a wolf."[14]

Despite a continual drizzle, on the morning of 29 June the launches and the punts went off under the orders of Tova with the empty water barrels. The earlier problem of substandard water supply had been remedied by the happy discovery of a stream, hidden from the previous reconnaissance, which permitted taking on better-quality water with greater convenience. By 2 P.M. the day's supply had been taken. Such was the accessibility of the spot that on succeeding days the task was repeated, with a change of officer each day, always with a sergeant and six armed soldiers, in addition to the armed sailors manning the boats. Even these precautions were not enough to prevent later that week the pilferage of two marlin spikes which were hung from the stay of the *Atrevida*'s mizzenmast. Chief Ankau, when advised of this occurrence, used his authority and eloquence fruitlessly in an effort at recovery.

This repeated propensity of the Mulgrave Tlingit for thievery, which seems to have been equally prevalent as their continual singing, resulted in a second suspension of trade aboard. Any exchanges were again to be carried out ashore. The Spaniards selected a place on the beach under the guns of the corvettes and in a totally open area, free of hiding places, groves of trees or shelter of any kind, characteristics that also made it the best site for the scientific observatory.

At first the natives went to the new location, but soon they attempted to return to the corvettes where they could enjoy greater profits in trading with the enlisted men, count on greater diversion amidst the hubbub of shipboard activity and hence have greater op-

These portraits of a Mulgrave Tlingit and his chief show details of native clothing. The chief's woven hat is decorated, while his subject's is plain. Pencil drawing by José Cardero. (Museo Naval MS 1725-11; Higueras 2931, Sotos 581)

portunity to steal. But shipboard trade was not re-established; rather the natives were compelled to go to the spot where the field tent had been set up for scientific study. One drawback of the native behaviour was the absolute need to return all scientific instruments aboard the vessels at night.[15] Even with the ceaseless rain, and a change of Spanish interest from furs to items for the Royal Bureau of Natural History, trade continued satisfactorily. The expedition's desire to add fresh salmon to the daily ration resulted in establishment of a set price of one three-centimetre nail for a salmon, for this "was the price of some exquisite fish of three kilograms which in Europe are viewed as provender of sumptuous tables, and in the port of Mulgrave became disdained by the sailors themselves."

On 30 June, early in the morning, the natives impatiently awaited the first rays of the sun in their efforts to visit the vessels and re-establish trade there. They brought new trade items and a great quantity of fish. Even the chief tried his hand at a previously offered line of commerce without success, attempting to obtain profit through prostitution of his female subjects.

The Spaniards were even earlier risers than the natives. Very early in the morning launches were sent ashore for water and the geographer, Bauzá, was dispatched in an appropriately well-armed boat to begin his geodetic survey from the harbour entrance to Point Phipps. Still another boat carried Juan Maqueda and his party to commence sounding the interior of the port. Malaspina and Cevallos went ashore to the nearby observatory, carrying the gear for checking the operation of the chronometers and to begin the various gravitational calculations which had been added to routine functions by royal order. Near the scientific observatory was a place two metres square,

covered with stones, and in which, according to the chief, were buried only the children of his family and those of another Indian who always accompanied him and apparently carried out the functions of minister of state. Three metres further on was another group of stones which covered the corpse of a warrior, "who achieved this honour for having died valorously in the latest encounter that they had with their enemies."[16]

In the late afternoon, during one of the few periods of really clear weather during the corvettes' stay, a beautiful panorama presented itself before the commanding officer, one that was both unexpected and grandiose. Becoming lyrical for the moment, Malaspina likened it to the sudden opening of the curtain at the theatre which presents at an instant to the amazed spectator a great number of both new and pleasant things. When the clouds and haze dissipated, the entire majestic cordillera from Mount Fairweather to Mount St. Elias, which had previously been obscured, could be seen. Moved by that spectacle, Malaspina wrote: "The snow with which they were covered from the peak to the final slope reflected the rays of the sun with a new brilliance; and there could be seen in the foreground of the higher land for some leagues distance all the pine forest with such luxuriance and abundance of leaves that it was difficult to describe. Finally, the exceedingly pure atmosphere with a soft breeze from the north, extending greatly the length of the day with such a great clarity of the twilight, even at midnight, did not deprive us of this pleasant and majestic view."[17]

News of the Spanish arrival was soon known beyond Mulgrave. On the same morning at 7 A.M. a sentinel that the natives left posted nightly at the entrance of the port advised of the approach of two foreign canoes. All of "the republic" became agitated by the news. Chief Ankau, after haranguing the populace, either in exhorting it to defend itself from the enemy, or to direct his people in their conduct with the new guests, came in haste, accompanied by one of the highest ranking sub-chiefs, to ask aid of the Spaniards. Both of them, with great earnestness and with evidence of true fear, announced the approach of the two native craft and their concern whether they were hostile or peaceful. While the two canoes were still about two or three kilometres from the anchorage, the two chiefs entreated the Spaniards to go out to the farthest beach and fire a rifle shot to force the approaching Indians to indicate their intentions. Meanwhile, all the Mulgrave natives made ready to fight. The women were evacuated, and two large canoes that had been beached were placed in the water. Since the Spaniards wanted to respond positively to the request of the local Indians, a group went off to the appropriate beach and at the proper moment for being seen and heard fired a single rifle shot. All of the natives who were manning the approaching canoe responded to the rifle fire by breaking forth into the inevitable song, which was, "as we believed," a peaceful sign and which resulted in most of the Mulgrave Indians returning to their former tranquility.

Suria later noted the Mulgrave's typical response to such a challenge.

Whenever some canoe from the neighbourhood whose Indians are subject to some other chief comes to this island they make a salute to it which is worth describing. As soon as they see them, they go down to the beach and all together in unison kneel until they remain on their knees, and on standing up, they utter a great cry, very ugly and ferocious, on a *gangora* which sounds something like an N. This they repeat three times and at the last they end with a very sharp and quavering shriek.

Chief Ankau was not so easily lulled into hospitality and continued to shout at the new arrivals "that they should look out what they were doing because we [the Mulgraves and Spaniards] were allies." The inbound canoes made directly for the corvettes, but when informed by Ankau that the chief of the foreigners was on the nearby beach at the observatory, the two canoes headed there. These craft were of equal capacity: each held "fifty men." In the middle of the first that arrived at the shore was a person, "whose grave aspect seemed to us to proclaim his authority, and we were convinced of it when we saw the Indians [ashore] throw themselves into the sea" to help the "August Prince" out of the canoe. This done, he was immediately presented to Malaspina by the Mulgrave chief.[18] Malaspina commented that in the final analysis "they seemed rather to all belong to the same tribe than to be persons who an hour earlier were prepared to destroy each other."[19]

In the afternoon, during another of the few breaks in the clouds, Mount St. Elias came into full view. That great climax peak for which the entire range is named, first seen by Commodore Vitus Bering in 1741, was measured for its elevation. The calculation was done from a distance of 41 leagues from its summit and resulted in 2,792 *toesas*,[20] therefore 887 higher than the normal Spanish reference peak of Tiede on the island of Tenerife in the Canaries.[21]

In the succeeding days other canoes also came, attracted by the opportunity to trade for Spanish nails and bells, more than out of curiosity to see the visiting ships and the many objects that were entirely unknown to them. They viewed the corvettes with indifference, a large vessel and a small vessel being all the same to them.[22] These visits increased the range of scientific collections by expanding the material culture items obtained beyond the Mulgrave Tlingits, but

Malaspina and his colleagues recorded no specific information on either who these visitors were or from how far they had come.

Operations and Observations in Port Mulgrave

Initial routine readings were made as follows: high tide was noted at 12:20 with the water rising two fathoms, while low tide was at 6 P.M. Fahrenheit temperature readings taken in the fresh air were: 8 A.M—55.3 degrees; 1 P.M—56.0 degrees; 4 A.M—47.0 degrees. One of the first priorities was to make use of various scientific instruments sheltered in the observatory tent, among them a simple fixed pendulum. This device was used to make gravitational calculations, such efforts being carried out in cooperation with French scientists and other European savants in an attempt to establish an international standard measure of distance. Officers José Espinosa and Ciriaco Cevallos, who had joined the expedition while it was in Acapulco, had been entrusted with delivering the proper equipment. These two newcomers were aware of the requirements for proper implementation of the experiment. One possibility was to establish an international standard of linear distance as the length of a pendulum which oscillated exactly sixty times per minute at sea level at the equator. Experiments were made at other latitudes and translated into an expression of that basic number, with both the anticipated and actual results being higher as distance from the equator increased. The experiments with the simple pendulum took approximately one hour after the apparatus was set up. While at Mulgrave, three separate sessions were carried out, all on 30 June. Six weeks later on 15 August while at Nootka, another session was completed, followed by two sessions on 19 August.

Although during the expedition hundreds of man-hours, two officers at a time, were spent in these calculations, it was to be wasted effort. In 1790, even before Malaspina began working with what to him was a new idea, a different standard was adopted for the metre, established as one ten-millionth of the earth's quadrant passing through Paris. One memento of the gravitational calculations survives in the form of a drawing of Malaspina and a fellow officer, perhaps Cevallos, sitting in the observation tent in full uniform while engaged in watching the pendulum. An associated experiment was to weigh a specific mass of material at such locations and to note the differences in weight at various latitudes. The recorded results were:

Acapulco 1000000
Monterey 1001070
Nutka   1002445
Mulgrave 1003823 [23]

As elsewhere during the voyage of observation and discovery, the visitors made an evaluation of existing timber resources. This was not done as a scientific detailing of botanical species, but rather as a practical listing. Shipbuilding and repair were primary considerations of these abbreviated "timber cruises." At various stops, both in those areas already known and those hitherto unknown, similar short lists of resources were made.

There is no evidence which officer or officers had the responsibility for these lists and brief descriptions. It may well have been a joint enterprise, though it is clear from the contents and presentation of these reports that, curiously, the knowledgeable natural scientist, Haenke, was not included.

Malaspina looks on as Cevallos starts the pendulum swinging, while another officer times it on the chronometer, part of an experiment to measure the earth's dimensions. The artist, Juan Ravenet, shows himself on the right making the sketch for this watercolour painting. (Museo Naval MS 1726-36; Higueras 2861, Sotos 71)

At Port Mulgrave the following list was made:

Timber of Port Mulgrave
1. Pine with smooth bark, white, light with few knots, streaked with considerable sap wood. The tree is very tall with little pitch. From its roots small seizing can be made. It has a white inner bark that the natives eat.
2. Pine with black, rough, fissured bark, light though not as much so as #1. It has some pitch and knots, and is hard to plane.
3. Pine with a thicker bark, rougher and heavier, with more pitch, more knots and a wider leaf. Frequently some of its fresh pieces won't float.
4. Pine like the mountain cypress. Thick, black, rough bark. This when cut from top to bottom can be used for oakum and for fishing lines. The roots of all these pieces serve for seizing, knees and all kinds of pieces for small vessels; and also for larger ones except for seizing.
5. Willow. Like that of Spain but twisted.
6. Alders that the Indians use for spoons, helmets and masks.
7. Wild hazelnut trees, but without fruit.
The Indians make fishing lines from the bark of the pine tree. The canoes that they make of this wood are 4.6 to 9 metres long and from 90 to 210 centimetres wide. They make other canoes of pieces tied together with a keel, stern post and stem, with frames and crosspieces and they navigate them preserving admirable symmetry for their tonnage. And the pieces are lashed together with pine fibres and then they line them with hides of_____ [the document ends abruptly at this point].[24]

The Malaspina visit to Mulgrave gave occasion to acquire some simple linguistic information. The officers were under orders to learn about the local languages, paying special attention to words that were most related to the expedition's needs. Although this approach was unsophisticated and lacked inquiry into the grammatical structure of Tlingit, it does represent an interesting non-commercial record. For

the Tlingit language, the Spaniards had no basis for comparison with lists made earlier by others. Malaspina's officers tried to equate native language sounds to Hispanic equivalents. At Port Mulgrave the first effort was with cardinal numbers resulting in the following:

tlecg or Klecg	=	1
teje	=	2
Nuzk	=	3
taajun	=	4
Keechin	=	5
Kletushu	=	6
tajatushu	=	7
Nuzkkatuschu	=	8
Kugshaco	=	9
chinkat	=	10

Suria was not as concerned with the Tlingit language as some of his colleagues, but did make the following comments:

Their language is very harsh. It abounds greatly in KK's and HH's. On board there are some who assert that it seems to be the tone of a monarch shouting wildly and in an arrogant and fearful tone. A curious man on board had the patience to put down some words, but he did not keep on because he thought it was impossible to transfer to paper such combinations of letters, some of which are impossible, such as "bg." An enemy they call *cuteg*, which they pronounce like one who is clearing his throat of phlegm. I have made out the following: *ankaiui* means Lord or superior; *chouut* means woman; *kuacan*, a friend; *tukriunegui* means a child at the breast; and *anegti*, a boy.[25]

The Spanish visitors also recorded several everyday terms:

Kaashegui	=	head
Kakac	=	forehead
Katcé	=	brow
Kaashiiu	=	nose
Kaujo	=	tooth
tizi	=	the sun's daily revolution
tlru	=	the land
Eu	=	the sea
Yn	=	the water
Anegueti	=	boy or girl
Shaut	=	woman
Koakan	=	friend
Sha	=	the snow
tuko	=	a canoe
Akan	=	the sun
Ancau	=	Lord or Chief
Aa	=	affirmation[26]

Song, as was repeatedly evident in the contact of Spaniards and Indians, was an integral part of Pacific Northwest Coast native life, and had accompanied the first introduction of Malaspina's group to Tlingit society. Song was used for greetings, in preparation for warfare, and for other special occasions. Using the special musical skills of Tadeo Haenke, the visitors recorded but did not translate a "Song of Happiness:"

ye aa Cl llakili kashláa (si namis) talli
(a breath is taken)
nake calayá o : aa :::: alayi o ye alay

Artist Suria was so impressed with one Tlingit song that he felt it useful to give an account of it:

Believing that we were very angry, they did not stop singing all afternoon and night and this song is interesting. They divided themselves into three parties each of considerable numbers and planted themselves on the beach in front of the ships. At the end of each song they finished with a kind of laugh which jointly and in measure they sustained on this sound Xa, Xa, Xa, Xa, Xa. In others they ended with another sound that cannot be described, but it was like the barking of a dog. Thus they went on all night, leaving us unable to sleep.

On the occasion of receiving foreigners, they make use of others [songs] of this style in order to ask for peace, as we found out as the result of having suspended with them for a day the commerce in skins.

Lieutenant Commander Tova also mentions the Mulgrave propensity for song on various occasions. He indicated that the natives pleaded a thousand times to come aboard the *Atrevida*, and perhaps with the idea of obtaining this favour they gave us several vocal concerts. The choirmaster kept time with a little paddle and sang his solos, subsequently singing in chorus and singing together in an outstanding manner. At the end of each stanza they raised their voices, they hunched their bodies down, they stamped vigorously on the deck, including all those gestures which usually depict anger and annoyance. I do not know if one can judge a musical work without great knowledge of the art, but one can claim that the Mulgrave songs pleased everyone. Nevertheless, though their music was used to seek or demonstrate peace, it rather reflects a savage character and is more appropriate to arousing martial passions rather than arousing sweet and tender sentiments. Our musicians went away at sunset without having come aboard, but rich with our presents and satisfied with our friendly conduct."27

The Act of Sovereignty

One motive for Malaspina's visit to the most northern latitude that he could reach was the important, seemingly indispensable, need to establish Spanish sovereignty over the area in advance of other nations attempting the same action. Sovereignty in international law involves the right to rule. During the colonial period this right was normally established through a symbolic act of possession. Over the years this legal ceremonial became a well-established ritual, performed hundreds of times until it became highly formalized.

It is useless to argue what moral right any European power had to establish its political control over aborigines of the New World or elsewhere. The assumption that European nations had that authority has held good almost everywhere, despite its obvious paternalistic basis which by present standards is unpopular. The only question seriously debated in Malaspina's time was whether an act of possession in itself created sovereignty based on the right of discovery, or whether discovery had to be perfected by effective occupation. European nations argued either or both sides of that question, depending on self-interest and on primacy of arrival, the fact of taking symbolic possession, and the details of later occupation or of neglect.

Spain had a second line of legal backing for its claims in the New World, one founded on the early Papal bull, *Inter caetera* of 3 May 1493, which divided the world between the two great Iberian maritime powers of the late fifteenth century, Spain and Portugal. This decree, issued by Pope Alexander VI, created a dividing line whereby each nation received half of the uncivilized world with the expectation that Christianization would ensue. Obviously, North European nations did not feel bound by such an edict from Rome. However, they all performed their own somewhat similar acts of sovereignty, except for elimination of the religious basis of the Iberian acts, being governed in their possessory formulas by a combination of ancient Roman law and medieval ritual.

The Northwest Coast became a test case for rights based on symbolic acts of sovereignty, on primacy of exploration, and on the intention of settlement. By the time of Juan Pérez's 1774 expedition to 55° north latitude, Spanish acts of sovereignty were both stereotyped and stylized, though Pérez failed to carry out his very specific instructions concerning possession taking. This failure was remedied in 1775 by the Hezeta-Bodega expedition which performed these rites at several places along the coast, setting the tone for subsequent similar Spanish acts of sovereignty.

The ritual as performed prior to 1791 was political, military and religious in nature. A large cross with appropriate inscriptions was prepared to be erected ashore at a prominent location so as to be visible at a considerable distance. A temporary chapel was prepared. A solemn Mass was sung by the expedition chaplain, a sermon was preached, a volley of artillery was fired, and a Te Deum and a God Save the King were included in a lengthy ritual. A long document, listing all of the titles of the King and many titles of the Viceroy, was prepared, signed by all the literate spectators, and notarized by the ever-present *escribano*, who made multiple copies. One copy was stuffed into an empty bottle, and after this feat was accomplished, a stopper and sealing wax protected the new contents. The bottle was buried at the foot of the cross which had been set deeply into the ground, and a proper volley of ships' cannons signalled completion of the formal event. It was a time-consuming, elaborate and well-rehearsed ceremonial reflecting both the religious and juridical bases for Spanish claim to sovereignty. Some efficiency was achieved by carrying a prepared form on which the explorers only needed to fill in the proper blanks, but even so, the entire ritual was a matter of hours rather than minutes.

The Malaspina visit provides a sudden break with earlier practice as regards establishment of sovereignty. Almost all of the ritual, including the strong religious orientation, was omitted, resulting in the much more streamlined version that was first seen at Yakutat Bay, Alaska.

At Mulgrave, once reprovisioning of water and wood was completed, launches were available in which the explorers could carry out what in the first place had attracted them to that particular area – inspection of the opening that seemed to offer some promise of the long-sought strait. Although professing doubts that this might be the Strait of Lorenzo Ferrer Maldonado, Malaspina wanted to examine those places and decide beyond all doubt such an important part of his commission.[28]

With supplies for fifteen days and enough water and wood, a small exploring party set out at dawn on 2 July, with command of the two launches being in the hands of Tova and of Malaspina himself. Also present were Bauzá and Pilot Joaquin Hurtado, and possibly Artist Cardero. Contrary winds made it necessary to spend considerable time at the oars, but once near the targeted opening a favourable wind commenced. At the same time the crews of the launches could see floating toward the western shore of the bay many large chunks of ice,

whereas to the east lay a stretch of flat land which, because it was protected from the north winds by the nearby mountains, gave evidence of being the refuge of some Indians, whose presence was also evident by smoke rising at different places.

Under difficult conditions, the launches made headway, and after passing some Indian huts, a lone Tlingit in a native canoe came out to greet the Spaniards. He was dressed in a most unusual manner, consisting of a cap, shirt, blue pantaloons and a blue jacket, part of a European uniform. He had earlier been introduced as the son of the chief whom the Spaniards called Ankau, the venerable head man at Mulgrave. The Spaniards thought that he had dressed that way to present himself as an old acquaintance of theirs.[29]

Whereas on previous occasions this young chief had not been very friendly during repeated visits to the corvettes, "with his new clothes, his customs appeared to have humanized a great deal."[30] Before, he had been the most arrogant and provocative of his tribe, but now his conduct bespoke gentleness and subordination, the causes for which the Spaniards found hard to understand. He went aboard the launch of the *Descubierta*, where he identified himself as chief of the nearby village and indicated that his wives and children were there. He consented to accompany the explorers in exchange for some trinkets and a meal of which "he had more than a little need."

The young chief quickly recognized the purpose of the scientists' visit, and by means of signs and even of a song, he seemed to them to be indicating that the opening that they were about to enter was completely closed at its far end. "The very little strength of the tide and all the answers given by the new Ankau convinced us not only that the desired strait did not exist in this area, but also that this canal was very short and that we had just about come to the end of it," wrote Malaspina. It was seen that to the west the interior shore was adorned by a permanent block of ice, which suggested that the area was closed. However, the overcast sky and the depth of soundings gave rise to some minor doubt.[31]

By 1 P.M., guided by the young chief, the launches were able to reach an anchorage inside the bay, one where there was a nearby stream, a bit of level land and the most promising appearance of vegetation. Except for these small places, noted Malaspina, "which could be properly called green stains, everything surrounding the bay was a mass of stone covered with ice."[32] The Spaniards noted evidence of a build-up of layers of ice in the many bergs that floated in their vicinity and which they heard calving with great noise from time to time from the nearby glacier. Even in the few places with vegetation, it seemed to the visitors impossible for the ice to melt in the rest of the summer.

Despite the continuation of cold, rainy weather, Bauzá established some landmarks, took a few bearings and made various observations. Tova was put in charge of hunting, and others set out to gather natural specimens which would later be turned over to Tadeo Haenke for his scientific examination. Meanwhile, their native guide cut out under the pretext of wanting to return home before nightfall and with the promise of bringing some fresh salmon the following morning. The exceedingly long summer days of northern latitudes allowed for extra hours of work but did not give the party members great opportunity for rest. They made every effort to extend their explorations as close to the icy edge of the bay as possible. It was obvious that the bay would not provide a refuge for large vessels and that it was not the sought-for strait. But a clearing and the good offices of some other local Indians who brought salmon gave the boat crews some rest.

A visual representation of this excursion exists in the Museo Naval in a colour drawing of the *Vista del Puerto del Desengaño* ascribed to Juan Ravenet, an artist who was not present but who later joined the expedition. It was doubtless originally by Cardero or Bauzá since the detail is much more after their style, but Ravenet was responsible for the finished product. Bauzá also drew a map of the area.

As a final episode of the junket, the act of sovereignty was performed and names were given to prominent geographical features. On 20 June 1791, the exploratory party stopped near the shore to perform the new act. The ceremony was reduced to gathering a great quantity of rocks, forming with them a pyramid and placing at its base a bottle, closed tightly with wax, containing a coin and a paper upon which Malaspina had penned the following words: "The Corvettes of His Majesty Descubierta and Atrevida commanded by Don Alejandro Malaspina and Don José Bustamante discovered this port on the 20th of June 1791 and called it Desengaño, taking possession of it in the name of His Catholic Majesty."[33] This was clearly a revised act of possession, with the coin and a brief note serving to establish all that the older rite had done. Despite these elaborate or simplified acts, and despite maintaining military settlements at Nootka and at Neah Bay, Spain never really exercised its right of sovereignty over this region. The native people were never considered to be Spanish subjects, no taxes nor tribute were ever collected, Spanish laws were never enforced upon the natives, nor were any of the other prerogatives associated with the juridical concept of sovereignty ever exercised. Had Spain stayed longer or if

Vista del Puerto del Desengaño en

Crews set out in the ship's boats to determine whether beyond the Port of Desengaño lay the fabled Strait of Anian. Watercolour by Juan Ravenet after a drawing by José Cardero. (Museo Naval MS 1726-73; Higueras 2932, Sotos 567)

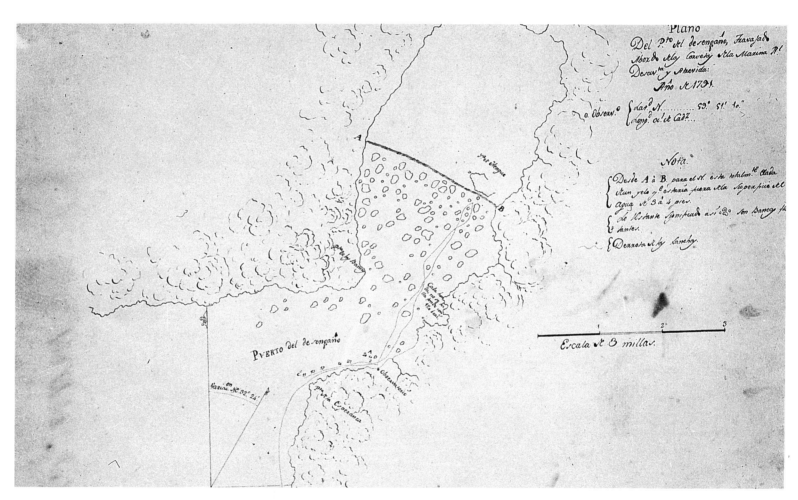

Instead of a passage to the Atlantic Ocean, at the end of the inlet lay a glacier calving ice floes into the North Pacific. (Museo Naval, Sig. IIB (3); Higueras 1722)

there had been no international challenge of its right to rule, events might have been quite different.

The Spaniards named the interior of the inlet Desengaño, the antonym of deceit, because both their doubts and hopes had been cleared away concerning the possibility of a strait. On modern maps it is translated as Disenchantment Bay. The island near which they anchored and near which they took possession was named Haenke in honour of the botanist "who shared with us on our voyage all the dangers and discomforts of sailing."[34] The entire opening was given the name Ferrer, "for the ancient mariner who actually motivated our inquiry."

One incident which demonstrates the inherent curiosity of these visitors was that, when the party was preparing its return to the corvettes at about 2 P.M., a man was discovered missing. Marine Gunner Manuel Fernández of the *Atrevida* had been last seen at 8 A.M., headed along the east side of the inlet for the purpose of examining it to its very end. It was a long and rocky distance, one that required crossing nearly inaccessible mountains covered with snow and inhabited by bears. Seeing the lateness of the hour, Fernández was almost given up for lost.[35] Malaspina ordered Lieutenant Tova to head a search for the missing crew member.

In a launch, and following the coast, the rescue party was amazed at the rugged country that he must have travelled. At last Fernández was spotted at a great distance. When he arrived at the launch, he was in such a state of fatigue that his condition lessened the anger that his rashness deserved. He had succeeded in going beyond the island named for Tadeo Haenke and had discovered a river that had been hidden from the view of the main party. Tova explained that "a deed of this sort, at first sight, deserving of punishment, merited through its circumstances the indulgence of the Commander, and is no less worthy that we mention here the honourable intention that brought it about." When in Acapulco, Fernández not only had deserted but also had induced others to commit the same offense;[36] as a result, he had lost his position as mainmast lookout. But the forgiveness of the Commandant and the officers had proposed to him that by means of a distinguished act, he could again merit his post as well as the confidence of his superiors. Fernández saw his self-appointed arduous task as a chance to regain his position. Such was the effect on his superiors of his intrepidity that he was forgiven and restored as lookout immediately upon return to the corvettes.[37]

With its work done, the reconnaissance party expected an easy trip back to the corvettes, but a change in wind forced them back to the oars and to a second visit to the village of Ankau's son, who was equally cordial as before, including bringing two of his very young children for a visit. The young chief showed himself to be an extremely loving parent, which motivated appropriate presents from the Spaniards. On their part, the natives gave the visitors many good-sized salmon.

From the vantage of the sheltered native village, the Spaniards were able to take bearings on distant Mount St. Elias, marked out a base line for mapping, and they did some sounding of the deep channel they had been navigating. They also took time to note the existence of many bothersome mosquitoes. Finally, after three days, the exploring group returned to the corvettes which meanwhile had continued their scientific labours, and had been engaged in limited trade with the Mulgraves, although all had not been harmonious.[38]

Problems at Mulgrave

During their stay in Port Mulgrave, the Spanish made a great deal of effort to maintain good relations with the natives, but this was achieved in large measure through fear of European firearms rather than any peaceful intentions on the part of a group which "by nature was warlike and ferocious." The Spanish felt forced to chastise the Indians for their breaches of decorum, an almost daily occurrence, following which attempts were made by both groups to reinstate good relations. During the absence of the launches in the interior area of Yakutat Bay, this precarious harmony degenerated somewhat, due in considerable measure to the weakened military strength of the visitors.

On 2 July, following departure of the launches, the rest of the small boats had continued taking on water and began cutting wood at a spot not far from the Mulgrave village. The officer in charge of the detail was trying to hasten the work as much as possible while at the same time taking precautions against any disorders. However, the natives, motivated by the "gentleness of our conduct, gave way to all sorts of excess when they judged our forces to be weakened by the absence of the launches." The orders issued by Cayetano Valdés to the wood cutting detail were not sufficient to prevent an Indian from stealing a sailor's clothing. Thinking that if he tolerated this offense, there would probably ensue a greater one, Captain Bustamante called the chief, whom he reproached about the conduct of his vassals, adding that it was absolutely necessary to return the stolen clothing. Chief Ankau excused his people, attributed the offense to the visiting foreign tribes, and failed to punish the delinquent. Tova records: "The robbery, considered in itself alone, was in truth a thing of little importance; but the robbery suffered diminished the opinion of our power and could have some fatal consequences. We still lacked a great deal for completion of our water and our wood; we had to continue our astronomical observations, etc., none of which was practicable if we could not count on the friendship, or better said, on the respect of these men."

The Spaniards felt that honesty was an attribute unknown among the Tlingit and that fear alone could contain them within the limits of justice. Under these circumstances, and avoiding violent measures, Bustamante agreed with the chief what prudence also dictated – that trade would be prohibited. This solution in a way achieved his objective because it resulted in the return of the stolen clothing, but it was insufficient to control the natives.[39]

Since by that earlier decision the natives were not permitted to board the corvettes, they all gathered where the wood cutting party was occupied, about a kilometre from the Mulgrave village. One native wanted to attack the Spanish sentinel who was guarding the clothing of the workers, and with a dagger he threatened Lieutenant José Robredo, who had to reprehend him for such conduct. This officer would not have been able to defend himself if it had not been for another Indian who intervened between them and foiled the designs of his compatriot.

Shortly thereafter Bustamante arrived along with many of the officers, and all engaged in some target practice "in order to demonstrate indirectly to the natives the terrible action of our arms and the superiority that they had over theirs." The same Indian who only a short time earlier had attacked Robredo now arranged a cured pelt of six thicknesses, and placing it in a convenient location, invited the Spaniards to fire at it from fifty paces. Lieutenant Cevallos was ready to fire when the Indian ordered that the test be postponed until he could take the pelt and submerge it in water six or eight times. Once it was wet to his satisfaction, he replaced it in the same position as before. "Fortunately, the ball penetrated the pelt through all of its thicknesses, carrying away part of the wood on which it was placed, and the Indians remained convinced that neither distance nor water could prevent the destruction of the burning fire of our thunderbolts."[40] The native who had proposed the test and whose theory of the impenetrability of wet fur was disproved was extremely angry over the results and went irately away from the scene of action.[41]

During a lull in other activities, Tomás Suria took advantage of the occasion to draw many of the activities and objects that he had been seeing. Valdés and Lieutenant Fernando Quintano examined the Tlingit arms and utensils and found many that they considered worth acquiring for the Royal Bureau of Natural History. The Mulgrave women were observed in sewing and the men in various activities of woodworking, making objects such as those that the officers and even the enlisted men had already eagerly acquired. Some of the other officers were occupied in recording new words and others in studying the domestic customs, all "displaying that constant love of science and of the work that has produced so much fruit for the expedition."[42]

At the place where they had been taking on water, everything went smoothly despite an increase in the number of natives present. From a nearby family, Lieutenant Espinosa had opportunity to learn of various domestic customs and to acquire a few items of the dress and adornment of the women.

"One event occurred aboard the *Atrevida* which had to cause us special amazement concerning the character of these natives," wrote Malaspina. It concerned a servant, a native of the Philippine Islands, whom the local Indians from the very first day believed to be one of their own people. They carefully examined his hair, his skin, his facial features, and even his limbs. They then asked that he remain with their tribe, and tried to find out how it was that he was with the explorers, whether he had been sold or captured.[43]

After a sortie around the area, Bauzá reported the land between the watering place and Point Muñoz as exceedingly luxuriant and the nearby fields so abundant with a type of wild strawberry that even his entire party of five sailors could not eat them all had they tried. On this excursion, the party also visited the burial place indicated by Dixon in the record of his earlier visit, a matter of considerable wonder. Bauzá felt that a visit there would do much to cast some light on the religious principles of those people.

Acting on Bauzá's report, on the following morning Artist Suria, José Espinosa and some other officers went in a boat to the river near which these objects of interest were located. Arriving at about 9 A.M., they chanced upon a group of four or five natives who were out gathering strawberries for food. These seemed to be of the lowest order of Mulgrave society and therefore little capable of satisfying the curiosity of the Spaniards. But since the excursion's purpose was to collect things for the Royal Bureau, they were perhaps more useful than any others, who out of reverence or out of fear would not have let the visitors have a free hand.

Suria provides an account of this sortie.

One morning the commander arranged for us to go in the boat to look at these monuments which no voyager had seen. We therefore went and saw the sepulchres in this form. A little bit away from the bank of the river, or

Chief Ankau stands aboard a canoe holding up a pair of seaman's trousers which had been taken, while another native makes the sign for peace. Bustamante had detained one of the chief's sons aboard the Atrevida and suspended all trading until the trousers were returned. Watercolour by an anonymous artist after a sketch by José Cardero. (Museo de América 2-259; Palau 54, Sotos 566)

Local Tlingit, keen to trade, cluster their canoes around the Spanish ships in the harbour at Mulgrave. Ink and wash drawing by José Cardero. (Museo de América 2-249; Palau 43, Sotos 557)

rather arm of the sea (because this enters into it and by signs the Indians gave us to understand that it divided the island and passed to the other side of the great sea), there is some undergrowth very fruitful in wild celery, camomile, like that in Spain, and many other herbs which I do not know, besides a great abundance of strawberries, so many in fact, that those who went were able to satisfy themselves, and many pine trees. Near these on the right hand side there were two square boxes raised from the ground 2 metres and held up by four pillars, also square. Of these boxes, that on the left side had on the face of it to the front various masks and other signs of which we do not know the significance. At the foot of the boxes, that is, on the surface of the ground, there are others, which were those that we explored and inside we found a calcinated skeleton between some mats. This box with all it contained we took on board.

Farther on along the same beach there is a skeleton house which is reduced to three frames, each one of three sticks placed parallel to each other at a proportionate distance, the one in the middle being higher than the other two. On the base of the poles which face inside there are various designs. The chief whom we found there made various signs to us which nobody could understand, but that we thought was that either before or after the funeral ceremonies they have a dance in this place, which must be of some particular significance, as after pointing out that they covered these piles with something, he took out his knife and stuck it into the stick and at once began to dance with a very happy gesture, making various movements and emitting an "O" from his throat. Some were of the opinion that it might be that, after some important victory against their enemies, they celebrated in this place, and they founded this opinion on his action in sticking in the knife.[44]

Malaspina indicated that a better idea of the burial places could be obtained from the drawings that he intended to publish in lieu of a difficult and tiring description.[45] It was noted that such burials were only for the chief and his family, something that seemed substantiated by a few pits covered with boards and stones, under which were coals, part of the family funeral pyre.

The Spanish prohibition of trade irritated the Mulgraves "in direct proportion to the value they placed on the Spanish trifles, of which we had proof as positive as it might have been fatal." Bustamante, along with fellow officers Francisco Xavier Viana, Fabio Ali Ponzoni and Manuel Esquerra, disembarked during the afternoon of the same day at the beach next to the Indian village. The natives, who were looking for an opportunity to engage in hostilities, or for some other reason which the Spaniards could not understand, carried off a young sailor and took him to their dwellings, at which time his absence was noticed by Lieutenant Viana. The native who was holding the sailor let go when the Spaniards shouted at him, and pulling out his knife, he ran toward Bustamante intending to wound him. He would have done so if four or five loaded shotguns had not prevented him. Instead, he shouted to his people, and instantly the Spaniards were surrounded by natives, each with dagger in hand blocking the way in every direction, and hardly giving the Spaniards enough room to use their shotguns. "These arms were, in truth, too weak a recourse, because once fired, it would not have been possible to reload them before being trampled by the crowd."

In these critical circumstances, the Mulgrave chief appeared, but he made no effort to contain the rebellious natives, either so as not to compromise his authority or because he was also operating in bad faith. But the chief's presence gave the Spaniards the break they needed in order to reach the shore. Once there, a first concern was to place their boat in the water, its crew consisting of four defenseless men. The party having gained a good position from which it could operate conveniently its firearms, it remained ashore more than an hour to show the Indians that their excessive numbers would never again be able to intimidate the Spaniards. A rapid retreat would have dissipated entirely the natives' opinion of Spanish power. "Nothing would have been easier than to carry out redress for what we had lost and to avenge the insult of this afternoon," recorded Tova, "but considering everything with judicious serenity, we returned aboard without causing the least harm, nor of later ordering anyone to do so."[46]

This occurrence made the Spaniards recall the sad fate of Captain Cook in the Hawaiian Islands, as well as that of the Viscount Sangre in the Navigator Group, and that of many other individuals of the unfortunate expedition of the Count of Lapérouse along the same coast of Alaska at Lituya Bay. These thoughts moved them immediately to advise the officers of the *Descubierta* of everything that had happened ashore, since they were at the point of going on a boat trip. It was thought prudent to return aboard, and on both corvettes new and stricter precautions were taken to ensure that in the future such scenes would not be repeated.

Soon the natives were lined up along the shore, singing various songs to ask for peace, "repeating in them several times the words *Atrevida* and *Descubierta*" in imitation of the way that the Spaniards passed the word from ship to ship.[47]

Artist Suria enlivens the account of 3 July with an incident which took place when he was left ashore alone with the Tlingits.

On account of my commission, and because the officers who accompanied me for the purpose of copying what was extraordinary and particular about their houses, had abandoned me, I saw myself in great peril in the house of the chief. I had scarcely commenced to work when with a great cry the cacique [chief] spoke to me in his language in an imperious tone and a threat that I should suspend my work. Engrossed in my work, I paid little attention to him when the third time there was a grand chorus of shrieks by all the Indians. I came to myself and suspended my work which was well started. They caught hold of me and pushed me. I began to shout for my own people, but when I turned my head, I did not see a single one. They formed a circle around me and danced around me knives in hand, singing a frightful song, which seemed like the bellowing of bulls. In such circumstances I resolved to carry out their mood and I began to dance with them. They let out a shout and made me sit down, and forced me to sing their songs which according to the gestures which they made I understood as ridiculing me. In such a situation I feigned ignorance and shouted louder, making the same contortions and gestures. They were very much pleased at this and I was able with my industry to gain their good will with a figure which I sketched for them with a coat, etc., and dressed like ourselves. They marvelled very much at this and began pointing at it with a finger, exclaiming "Ankau! Ankau!," which is to say "Señor [Lord]," as they call their chief. So they quieted down and insisted on giving me fish to eat. I excused myself as much as I could, but seeing that they threatened me, I had to eat. Soon they offered me some women, pointing out some and reserving some others for me. Seeing that I did not move, they made signs to me with their hands that they were giving them to me so I might violate them. At this moment a sailor arrived who was looking for me, since the boat was going aboard. I complained to some of the officers that they had abandoned me and they excused themselves by telling me that the natives who had remained on the beach were peaceable and that therefore they had inferred that they would not do me any harm. I forgot to say that as soon as they saw the sailor, they believed that more were coming and I took occasion of the opportunity to slip away.[48]

On 5 July deteriorating Spanish-Tlingit relations reached their lowest point. Versions vary concerning the sequence of events on the last full day at Mulgrave, but the general tenor of happenings echoes earlier scenarios. Tova indicates that as a result of the latest events involving the natives, the Spanish attempted to cut off all communication with the beach, "but nothing was more important than to observe the status and operation of the chronometers,"[49] particularly in view of the fact that this was necessary in order to rectify the longitudes of their most recent campaign and to make certain any subsequent positions. For this purpose, Lieutenant Juan Vernacci had been sent ashore to make observations using a quarter-circle. According to Suria, Vernacci had signaled from land that he was preparing to take the observatory aboard, but his message had been misunderstood as a request for assistance against the Indians, who had been insolent. In his account, Tova says that Vernacci advised the ships that the natives were restless, manifesting ideas of attacking the corvettes, and that they had deployed themselves along the nearby beach.

Captain Malaspina immediately gave an order to arm the men and to make ready the cannon. Malaspina, Valdés, Tova and four well-armed soldiers set out for shore, arriving at the place where the Indians had formed their party, setting at naught their lives in an attitude of defiance. The arrival of the Spanish forces, "far from containing, seemed to inflame more the ferocity of the Indians." One even drew his dagger and stood angrily in front of Valdés, who was armed with his shotgun and backed up by eight or ten other men with firearms.

At this moment, Malaspina ordered a cannon salvo from the *Atrevida*. The explosion frightened the natives. They covered themselves with their fur clothing and looked around to see who had fallen, but when they realized that the damage had not corresponded to the noise, they continued with their ideas of attacking. They deployed themselves in the shelter of the trees, armed with lances, with the apparent plan of doubling back and then attacking the Spaniards from the rear. Despite these obviously hostile intentions, the Spaniards succeeded in getting their instruments into the boat, and, with them, all returned safely aboard "without suffering or causing the least harm." The head of the water-gathering detail which was in progress and consisted of eight soldiers, being unable to determine the true motive of the cannon shot, speeded up his crew's movements, and by 2 P.M., they returned aboard with the launches and punts.

Meanwhile, at the anchorage, and probably having some effect on the outcome of what the Spaniards considered a "discord," the mariners had the advantage of having aboard the *Atrevida* as visitors Ankau and one of his sons. They had been brought there by one of many canoes that had earlier in the day surrounded the corvettes, but that gradually disappeared as the morning wore on. When events took a bad turn ashore and after the firing of the cannon shot, Captain Bustamante seized the two Mulgrave leaders and threatened to punish them if Ankau did not order his Indians to settle down. The chief's suggestion was that he be permitted to go ashore to quiet down his people, who were calling to him to save himself by jumping overboard and swimming ashore. Since neither his suggestion nor that of his people were very likely to be realized, he requested that the Spaniards not aim at the village where the women and children were located and directed his natives to lay aside their arms.

This had the desired effect, as with great shouts from on board, he commenced to hold back his men, who were uneasy and very anxious to come to blows with our people. In spite of the voice of their chief whom they saw a prisoner, they came very near to attacking us, having collected a considerable body of the Indians of this island. One of them scarcely saw the movement than he ran along the beach and put himself in front

A Spanish exploring party is shown conversing with natives near a memorial to a deceased chief. His remains would have been placed in a burial box behind the carved crest suspended high between the poles. Ink and wash drawing by José Cardero. (Museo Naval MS 1726.67; Higueras 2924, Sotos 559)

of them with his dagger, attacking Don Juan Vernacci and the whole body of our people. It would have been very easy to finish off all of them with such advantageous arms as guns and pistols which they had in their faces while defending the embarkation of the rest and fronting the enemy.[50]

Chief Ankau's son at the time of the cannon shot had grasped his dagger, so he had been tied up. Even when the chief was placed at liberty, his son did not want to accompany him.

Once ashore, Chief Ankau was "received with a thousand demonstrations of joy" by his people.[51] In evidence of his incomplete understanding of the reason for Spanish unhappiness with his people, Ankau thought that all the trouble was the result of one of the Indians having stolen a pair of trousers, an incident that had happened days earlier. The chief had obtained the purloined pants from its new owner. Suria wrote, "it was something to laugh at to see him in his canoe giving the sign of peace while hoisting aloft the pants" in an effort to restore good relations, particularly trade activity.[52] Ankau directed his efforts to Malaspina on the *Descubierta*, and peace was conceded as requested. The return of the stolen pants is depicted twice in the artistic archive of the expedition. One is an unfinished scene showing four native boats and a Spanish war vessel. The second, a colour enlargement of the centre of the foregoing scene, is an unusually interesting drawing entitled "Chief of Mulgrave asking peace of the Corvettes," and contains fine detail of that interesting moment as captured by expedition artists. Although the Spaniards thought that the natives were of such incomparably changeable character, possibly the Indians felt that the Spaniards were equally foolish in the number of times they became pacified by the simple singing of songs and signs of peace.[53]

Once again peace was restored, with the result that the Mulgraves laid aside all their fierceness and came alongside "very contented in their canoes, as if nothing had happened."[54] It was trade as usual.

The Mulgrave Tlingit

In summarizing his many contacts while at Mulgrave, Antonio de Tova, second-in-command of the *Atrevida,* gives us a long description of the natives. Although his service record shows him to be a man of moderate talent and somewhat lethargic, he was singled out as a person with infinite patience, a good capacity for primitive languages and a well-attuned ability at observation. Tova was the closest thing to an ethnographer aboard the scientific expedition vessels.

The stature of the Tejunenses (the name by which the inhabitants of Port Mulgrave are known according to our latest information) is at least equal to that of the Spaniards, and they are built proportionately, with the exception of the thighs and the legs, where the musculature is not as complete as in the rest of the body. Generally, they have a round face, a large mouth, large tightly-spaced teeth, a wide nose and small but black and brilliant eyes. Their hair, which they ordinarily wear tied with a cord around the crown of the head or loose down their backs, is lustreless and thick. In some it appears brown, which colour results from the combination of black, which is its natural colour, with that of some materials that they mix into it, the usage seemingly being exclusive among the most distinguished or older people.

Customarily the men of twenty-five years of age are without the least sign of facial hair, but after middle age, they have it long and thick. And this sudden change cannot be ascribed to nature, which observes in its works a regular progression, but seemingly in that they pull it out up to a certain period of life, and let it grow when authority requires it, or when

Despite Spanish determination to avoid conflict, a clash of attitudes over ownership of property led to a skirmish between natives and visitors. From an ink and wash drawing attributed to Tomás de Suria. (Museo Naval MS 1723 (6); Higueras 2927, Sotos 564)

Indio de Mulgrave

Detailed sketches such as this, one of many which make up the record of the expedition, are a rich source of ethnographic information. Ink and wash drawing by José de Cardero. (Museo Naval 1725-1 (2a); Higueras 2929, Sotos 578)

efforts at beauty cease. The Tejunenses, according to the common practice of all savages, paint themselves red, black and other colours, with which they increase their normal ugliness. We had some of them wash themselves to ascertain their true colour, which of their faces is as white as the people of south Europe, but of their bodies is much darker. Painting, the use of which is immoderate and continual, perhaps preserves the face from the rigours of the winds and the sun to which the Mulgraves are continually exposed.

The features of the women are as ugly as those of the men, there being nothing easier than confusing the two sexes, which are not set apart by any special form of dress. That of both consists of a tunic of natural or of cured skins which they usually equip with a collar and a hem of the same sort along the bottom. Over this tunic they place another cape of skins that they tie with cords across the chest, leaving free use of their arms. Among all customs that have been introduced by the caprice and extravagance of women in their desire to look good, there is none more unique than a special one of the Tejunenses women. They make an incision inside the lower lip parallel to the mouth and of the same length, and in it they place an elliptical shaped piece of wood, the length of which could not be less than five centimetres by two and a half centimetres wide. This piece is concave on both sides and its entire circumference is rounded where it fits and is secured to the lip. Once in place, by its own weight it assumes a horizontal position, and forcing the lip to separate from the mouth, all of the teeth of the lower jaw are left uncovered. One cannot imagine exactly how much an adornment that adds a thousand charms in the eyes of Tejunenses disfigured the face of these women. How different are the opinions of men concerning beauty!

After the events already referred to and various others, there is no doubt that supreme command is vested in the chief and that his position is hereditary in his family. We also noted other subaltern authorities, being able to assert that inequality of rank, so contrary to the simple and primitive state of nature, was in practice among the Mulgraves. But this difference in authority cannot come from the difference in wealth among men whose necessities are so limited and whose means of satisfying them are equally so.

This Tlingit frontlet, decorated with one of the owner's family crests, would have been worn on the head on ceremonial occasions. (Náprstek Museum, Prague 21.373)

The Tejunenses, as a natural consequence of their way of life, should be wanderers, but once established where hunting and fishing provide abundant subsistence, they make of those places their fixed abode. Necessity has not forced them to invade foreign territory, but they have to defend their own, and this necessity has made them great warriors. Their customs, their music and their dances all reflect a warlike character, and there is nothing of which they are more jealous than of their military reputation. They told us enthusiastically of their battles, they showed us their wounds, and they were infuriated when we showed a preference for our arms over theirs. Among the many that they use in their wars, both offensive and defensive, are the lance, the arrow and the knife, which is commonly used by them normally hung from a shoulder belt, and in battle they tie it with a strong thong to their wrist and prefer to lose their life rather than this terrible weapon. These knives, the normal length of which could not be more than five centimetres, are of local manufacture; and our conjectures have been many on the way that the Tejunenses acquired iron. Captain Dixon, who was first and after whom we were next in the discovery of Port Mulgrave, could not have supplied this metal so abundantly, and the perfection with which they work it is proof that its use is from a very remote period, with it not being improbable that it is found on the land of the continent next to these islands.[55]

In addition, Artist Suria wrote his impression, and since this was independent of the official accounts, it is of some importance, though Suria did not have any training as a natural scientist. He did, however, liberally intersperse his journal with rough sketches of the Tlingit. In his account he said:

I proposed to give a description of the Indians at Port Mulgrave; this I shall do now with the greatest brevity possible. In the first place they are of medium stature, but robust and strong. Their physiognomy has some resemblance to that of all Indians, except that their eyes are very far apart and are long and full. The face is rounder than it is long, although from the cheeks, which are very bulging, to the chin, it is somewhat more pointed. Their eyes are sparkling and alive, although always manifesting a wild and untamed air, a consequence of the methods by which they are brought up. They have little beard, although there is no general rule about this as I have seen some with a very full one. This and the hair of their head is so thick that it looks like the mane of a horse. The women have the same facial characteristics and if it were not for the red ochre and black soot which they put on, some of them would not be very ugly, although in general I would not venture to say that they were good looking. All of them, men and women, generally speaking, have something of Chinese features.

Their dwellings or habitations are very poor. Here can be seen their disorderly filth, for they are more like pigsties than the habitations of human beings. This causes such a fetid and disagreeable odour on their belongings and persons that you cannot stand it. The houses are on the bank of the sea at the point which the channel for leaving the port forms. They are of boards placed over the trunk of a tree without any order. This traverses it and forms the ridge pole on which the boards rest on one side and the other, the tree trunk being held up by others, perpendicular ones, sunk in the ground. On the top of the roof all their belongings can be seen, canoes made, others in skeleton, skins half-cured, wood, and other various rubbish. Inside you see the same. What cannot be put outside is put inside.

Here you can see some square wooden boxes. All their ornamentation is reduced to a mask on the four fronts with the mouth open, badly carved with the teeth inverted, and in others by way of ornament they have placed them in a parallel line. In another place you can see a great quantity of fish, which seemed to us like our conger eel, curing at the fire, and hanging on some sticks. In the same way they treat their salmon. Many skins are hung about, bows here, arrows there, knives, cuirasses, bundles of clothes; many children, all naked, and some men, other suckling children in their cradles, the women at their work, so that everything appears in the greatest confusion. They are always eating and heating themselves at the fire in the middle of the hut.

A native winter house at Mulgrave. Indians of the Northwest Coast moved from one village to another seasonally according to migrations of fish and marine mammals. When they moved, they took the planks that formed the walls and roofs of their houses with them, leaving behind the heavy timber supports. From an ink and wash drawing by José Cardero. (Museo de América 2-250; Palau 44, Sotos 558)

Their sustenance and daily meal is as follows: They catch a fish and pass a stick through it from the tail to the mouth and which they fasten in the ground. They keep turning it toward the fire. As soon as it is softened, they place it in a straw basket which is very flexible and is so closely woven that not a drop of water can come out. In this they put it to cook with sea water, and so that the basket may not burn underneath they have various red hot stones which they throw inside, as necessity demands, always maintaining the heat until the dried fish in small fragments forms a mess and then they eat it with some long deep spoons made of horn. I do not know to what animal the horn belongs because there are no bulls, cows, horses, burros, mares or other animals among the Indians, nor do they know of them.

When the Indians are newly-born they put them in a cradle made of a kind of reed, very well worked. Two skins hang down from each side of this which they fold over the breast of the baby and which covers it down to the knees. These are joined by a skin which through various holes extends from one side to the other. The babies are dressed with their arms inside, all with skins; thus they put them inside the cradle, and cover them very well down to the feet, as stated. Thus they manage the affair, giving them to suck and leaving them stretched out on the ground. As soon as they are born, they pass a very delicate feather through the cartilage of the nose for the purpose of making a hole in it, and in consequence the hole gets bigger, so that when they are grown they can put a nail of considerable size through it, which they do, as they all have holes in their noses.

The women, in addition to the hole in their nose, make one in their lower lip, horizontally, in which they place a roll of wood of elliptical form, hollowed out on one side and the other, and thick enough to hold it between the teeth and the lip. The size of it appears incredible, as well as the custom of wearing it. Clasping this roll with the lip, they talk, eat and do everything. We do not know if this is distinctive of the married women, although to me it seems so, because I have not noted it in other than these, and the unmarried ones do not use it. All of them tattoo their arms and hands in lines of various design and so remain forever. The dress of the women is very modest. It consists of a robe of tanned skin without hair, which covers them from their throat down to their feet, and the breast, and the arms down to the wrist. There is a sleeve which is wide but modest. In all, this tunic has the same form as that which they put on the effigy of Jesus Nazareno and tie around the waist. Besides this robe, they wear a cape or square mantle also of skin which is held on the right shoulder by a piece of leather, and some living on the banks of the sea wear a fringe. Some use these cloaks made strictly of marten skins.

The dress of the men is as I have stated, of various skins, the most common being that of the black bear, and very hairy. When it rains and they have no hats, they cover their heads with the same skin of the head of a bear, which makes them look like Hercules. The rest of the skin they gather in at the waist by means of a piece of leather and what is left of the animal, claws and tail, etc., hangs down to the middle of the leg. From this may be inferred that the arms, breast, stomach and belly are uncovered except the shoulders and the rump. In order that this skin may not get loose, they sustain it on the right shoulder by means of another connecting piece of leather. Some besides this wear another skin which we can call a cape or cloak, as it serves the same purpose. Others go entirely naked except for a breech clout. Their hair is loose (among the women also) but groomed with more care on one side than on the other, leaving the part of their hair uncovered, but covered with red ochre, and their faces painted with it, which makes them look horrible.[56]

With the intervention of an Indian who demonstrated the use of native arms and armament, doing so by signs made to the Spaniards, Suria was able to record and even make some sketches of the Mulgrave warrior.

The fighting Indians wear all their arms, a breastplate, back armour, a helmet with a visor or at least what serves that purpose. The breast and

This ink sketch from Tomás de Suria's personal diary shows the wood-slat armour the Tlingit used in battle. The detail at right shows the crest figure on the frontlet. (Bienicke Library, Yale University)

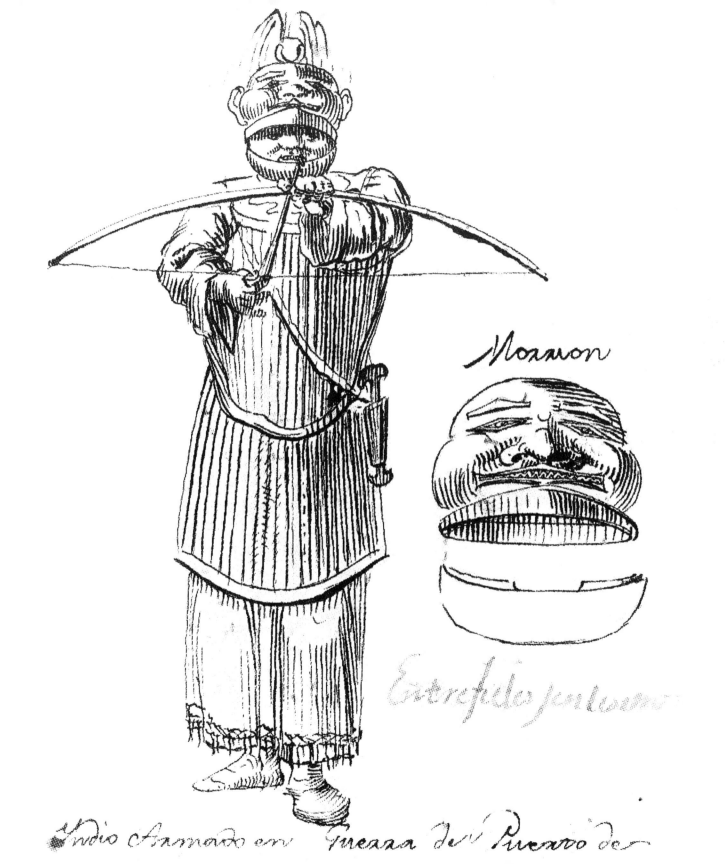

Mormon

Yndio Armado en Guarra del Puerto de

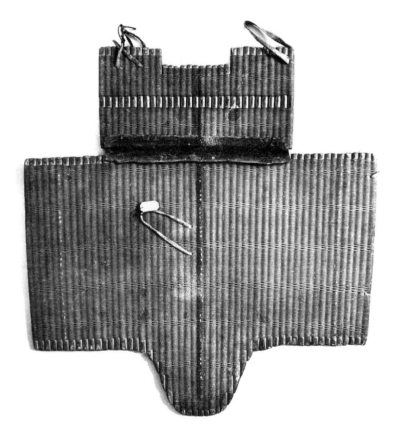

This preserved set of armour demonstrates the faithfulness and accuracy of Tomás de Suria's sketches. (Museo de América 13.883)

back armour are a kind of coat of mail of boards two fingers thick, joined by a thick cord which, after they are adorned both front and back, joins them with much union and equality. In this junction the thread takes an opposite direction, it being the case that even here the arrows cannot pass through, much less in the thickest part of the boards. The breastplate is bound to the body in the back. They wear an apron or armour from the wrist to the knees of the same character which must hinder their walking. Of the same material they cover the arm from the shoulder to the elbow, and on the legs they use some leggings which reach the middle of the thigh, the hair inside.

They construct the helmet of various shapes; usually it is a piece of wood, very solid and thick, so much so that when I put one on it weighed the same as if it had been of iron. They always have a great figure in front, a young eagle or a kind of parrot, and to cover the face, they lower from the helmet a piece of wood which surrounds this and hangs from some pieces of leather in the middle of the head to unite with another one which comes up from the chin. They join at the nose, leaving the junction as the place through which to see. It is to be noted that before they put this armour on they put on a robe like that of the women, but heavier and thicker, and with certain kinds of embroidery.

They hang a quiver and the bow they put over their arm, from which it hangs back of the shoulders. They clasp a short lance, a knife and a hatchet. Such is the equipment of a warrior. The lance is a heavy stick of black wood, very well worked, and at the point they tie on the blade of a great knife which they obtain from Englishmen in exchange for skins. The knife which they carry in their belt is the same as ours for the same reason. The hatchet is a black stone of the size, figure and edge of our iron hatchet. They fasten it to a heavy stick and make use of it in war and in their other necessities. The bows and arrows are the same as those of all other Indians.[57]

Switching to another aspect of Tlingit material culture, Suria indicated that there was very little household furniture in the native homes.

For their children they make some heads of marble for them to play with. They gamble with some little sticks, about eight or nine fingers long, and a finger in thickness, very well made. They count up to fifty with various signs, which differ one from the other. They shuffle them and then stretch one or two on the ground. From what we could make out, the companion must pick out from these two the one which has been hidden by the person doing the shuffling, which he recognizes by signs. If he succeeds, the little sticks pass to his companion and if not, the same man continues the same shuffling. There is sufficient reason for thinking that with this game they wager their persons and whoever loses has to be at the disposition of the other, because one of our sailors went to play with one of them, and having lost as usual, because he did not know the game, the Indian became very contented and made a sign to the sailor to embark in his canoe, because he was now his, and on being resisted, the Indian insisted, indicating by signs that he had won.

The pots and jars in which they cook are those already referred to. Their food consists of fish: salmon, smelts and another which looks like a conger eel.

We could not find any trace of their religion although to me it appears that they bestow some worship on the sun. I am of this opinion because in order for the chief to make us understand that our commander was taking observations on shore, he told us that Ankau (which is the same as Lord), our commander, was looking at Ankau. Therefore, if his word means superior, as so they name their chiefs, and the same word is used to speak of the sun, it seems possible that they are rendering it adoration. In their burials they keep some system and put up monuments to the posterity of the good memory of their dead.

Moving his attention to Mulgrave boat transportation, the artist had the following comments:

They use canoes of different sizes. The ordinary ones are of wood shaped like a weaver's shuttle and of this figure [which he drew]. Others are of skin sewed to a framework of poles, well constructed and tied, and are like this [of which Suria provided the figure]. The two holes in the centre are for entering. Half the body from the waist down is inside and they seat themselves on their heels as is their ordinary custom, and thus they manage the canoe with the oars. They use no rudder and in order to keep going straight they paddle the same number of times first on one side and then on the other with great speed. Their oars are very strange and are painted like the canoes with various marks and masks. They have some leather thongs which pass through the entire deck of the canoe and are tied on the sides. These are like stay rods where they put their lances and arrows and their oars when they are moving along.[58]

Whereas anthropologists and some early Alaska historians have suggested that prostitution was not known among the Tlingits at an early date, the preponderance of the evidence from as early as Malaspina's visit indicates the contrary. From the very moment of arrival, the local chief had offered the sexual use of his female subjects. Tova recorded that "at first we believed that only the women of the lowest class prostituted themselves, but we soon learned that even the least complacent member of the royal family would have sold her utmost favours for very little. The orders to prevent abuses of this type were very strict, and we can testify that they exactly fulfilled that purpose."[59] In addition, Suria's story of having been left alone and subject to ridicule and embarrassment in the house of the Mulgrave chief concluded by his saying that he had been provided with a group of women with whom he was invited to have sexual relations.[60]

In his summary account of the round-the-world expedition, Malaspina went into detail on the matter of Mulgrave prostitution, and from it there can be little doubt.

The repeated signs that they had made to us since yesterday of making available the use of their women once we were in port, although quite clear, seemed to us still mistaken and perhaps badly interpreted, bearing in mind the limited contact that the place had with European vessels and the strangeness of such an offer, since it was not motivated by either veneration or affection for us, nor from some customs altered by luxury, self-interest and example. One of our officers who at that time found himself not very far from the huts and pestered again by that sort of offer, wanted to make sure of its true meaning, because if that facility really did exist as we supposed, it was important to take precautions for the good order of our crews in their first contacts; and if it were not true, we should dispel this evil idea of their character and customs. Consequently, led by two young natives who with a mysterious appearance repeated to him the already known word *Shout* [women],[61] he drew close to some trees nearby the huts and then it was easy to dispel any doubts whatsoever, since, in fact, there were at the foot of a tree four or five women, half-covered with sealskins and obviously obedient to the will of almost the entire tribe, which seemed unanimous in its intention of prostituting them. Whatever out of morality and good example might not be achieved in turning one's attention away from all ideas of this kind, it would certainly have been achieved by their horrible appearance, and by the great amount of grease and filth with which they were covered, giving off an odour difficult to describe for its unpleasantness.[62]

Perhaps nationalistically, Malaspina speculated that these offers of prostitution were one of several vestiges of Dixon's earlier visit in the *Queen Charlotte*. The Spanish scientist felt constrained to reproach seriously the old chief on the occasion when he brought a woman toward the campaign tent in an effort to entice the officers. He also reissued orders that individuals other than the officers were not to go near the Indian huts. This in no way deterred the Indians, and about 6 P.M. there was seen near the stern of the *Descubierta* a canoe with three women, two of whom were not over eighteen or twenty years of age. Those Indians in the canoe repeated some English words, then broke into a long discourse in Tlingit, and finally broke into a quite

melodious song which Haenke "copied with his innate accuracy and understanding of music."[63]

Departure from Mulgrave

On 5 July, a decision was made to leave Mulgrave in order to take advantage of the summer months in the hope of completing the difficult assignment which lay ahead. Tova captured some of the last moments of the Spanish visit at Mulgrave:

Since our supply of water and wood was complete, and having carried out our experiments with the pendulum, corrected the movement of the chronometers, and drawn the chart of the port, there was no longer any reason to stay on. So from 7 P.M. on, we began the task of weighing anchor. The natives, knowing that our departure was approaching, hastened trade, many of them giving up even the furs in which they were dressed. Since they preferred clothing to other items that we offered, including iron, our sailors sold a great part of their baggage, and even some of the officers gave some clothing for which they no longer had use ashore or was unsuitable for the cruise, almost all of which was quickly traded to the natives, who were now easy to confuse with our Filipino sailors. Others were seen in complete uniforms and some with coats of fine cloth, buttoned down the front like us, and with the rest of their bodies unclothed.

At 8 P.M., with the tide halfway down, we set sail with a light westnorthwest [315°] wind. This was the moment at which the natives redoubled all their efforts to sell the final items and also at which we tried to show our friendship and generosity to many of them, which gave rise aboard the *Descubierta* to an interesting scene. The surgeon, Don Francisco Flores, gave some trifles to an Indian girl who had in her arms a nursing baby, on whose behalf she was going to trade a piece of fur; but when he [Flores] indicated to her that they were a present intended for the child, this tender mother, folding up the pelt and placing it over the head of the child, sent it to Flores as if in the child's name. After these first presents, others followed on both sides, as the generosity of the woman tried to compete with that of our physician. This contest would have been endless if Flores had not been obliged to follow his countrymen as they now moved away from the canoes. With her arms, the Indian woman demonstrated her friendship, as did the [other] natives who repeated the words *Atrevida* and *Descubierta*. The people of Port Mulgrave went off to their respective rancherias and the foreigners went off to round Cape Muñoz.[64]

Malaspina also penned his impression of the temporary impact that trade had on the Mulgraves and their neighbours. "It was, nevertheless, a unique and curious spectacle to see at that time a good half of the old tribe [Mulgraves] and some of the new [visiting] tribe dressed so strangely with old uniforms of the soldiers, seamen's jackets, caps, handkerchiefs, shirts, trousers, etc., both winter and summer wear, so much so that it would have caused the greatest surprise for any ship that they might go aboard, and probably make it suspect that the crew of a Spanish ship had been assassinated in the vicinity."[65]

Upon departure from Port Mulgrave, Lieutenant Ciriaco Cevallos on the Corvette *Atrevida* took pen in hand to summarize the stay in a patriotic and self-congratulatory entry in the Guard Book.

Thus after a short stay, but one fruitful of interesting events, we abandoned these rustic places with the sweet satisfaction of not having produced the least prejudice to its inhabitants. They always received double the price for their trifles, with order, equity and justice governing our actions. We respected their customs, and we patiently suffered their thievery, their bad faith, and their insults, and what is more oppressive the sentiments that stimulate anxiety for self-preservation, compromising our lives many times to avoid the shedding of blood as happened on the afternoon of the 3rd [of July]. This conduct, so in conformity with the beneficient and humane character of the Spaniards, will some day confound a certain class of writers who have dedicated themselves to defaming an illustrious and honourable nation that, despite their ridiculous and extravagant statements, will always occupy a distinguished place in the annals of the universe. If these reflections seem out of place in a book dedicated to writing with simplicity of a certain kind of events, this liberty should be pardoned to a person who in the most distant surroundings cannot lose sight nor forget the interests and opinions of his native land.[66]

These congratulations were premature. On the afternoon of 5 July at 6 P.M., both vessels weighed anchor for departure bound for Prince William Sound. When they were just about clear of any obstructions to navigation, and only a pistol shot from the port side of the channel, the *Descubierta* ran aground in two fathoms of water, its bow stuck between some rocks. The confusion caused by such an unexpected accident was great, but by the combined means of a kedge anchor astern, the longboat of the *Atrevida* under Lieutenant Viana, and its own boats, the corvette was towed off the rocks in a little more than an hour of effort. The result of Malaspina hanging his ship on some rocks was not great, for the damage was slight, and the only drawback was a delay of departure until very early the following morning at 3:30 A.M. with the outgoing tide, though even that was attended by great difficulty in shipping aboard the kedge anchor on which they had been riding.[67]

The Malaspina visit to Port Mulgrave in Yakutat Bay had been a period of much activity. The bay did not produce the greatly desired passageway to the Atlantic, but the area became a target for scientific study and collection of material for later incorporation into the body of material produced as a final result of the expedition.

Along the Alaska Coast

After a slow start getting under weigh from Port Mulgrave and difficulty in clearing Point Muñoz, the corvettes were favoured for a while with good weather. It was quickly determined that there was nothing visible that conformed in any way to the fabled Strait of Ferrer Maldonado. To the contrary, everything was totally inconsistent, which led Malaspina to decide that the ensuing weeks could be best spent in making a contribution to hydrography. Several chances to view and chart the coast were offered, but a change in weather finally made it advisable to head in haste to Prince William (Príncipe Guillermo) Sound, a place already known from the accounts of Cook and of several Spanish mariners who had been there earlier and had bestowed a series of place names. Some of these toponyms were soon erased, while others were translated from English into Spanish. A special matter that called the group's attention was the existence or non-existence of a reef reported by both Ignacio Arteaga and Bodega and called by them the Bajo de Pamplona.

On 8 July 1791 the corvettes lost sight of land, but they regained visual contact the following day when they sighted Cape Suckling (translated Cabo Chupador) and the Island of Kayes (spelled various ways by the explorers, and now called Kayak Island). At no time during this phase of the expedition did the corvettes anchor in any protected area, though occasionally they anchored out in the stream, motivated to do so by contrary weather, or by need for rest from the fatigue involved in maintaining even close to their desired course. They had wanted to enter Controller Bay, but after holding position for an entire night, they were unable to do so.

En route to their destination of Prince William Sound, the vessels passed the Ensenada de Menéndez, the Islands of Magdalena (Hinchinbrook), Montague and Triste (Seal Rocks) and sighted Cape Hinchinbrook (Inchinbrook to the explorers),[1] which they retitled by

Vista de la Ensenada de la Cruz demorando A. al N 17 E. dist.ª 11 millas. B. al N 68.° E dist.ª 9 millas, por la mañana tiempo acelasado

Vista del Puerto de los Remedios demorando el Punto A. al N 46.° E. distancia 9½ millas

*Drawn by Felipe Bauzá, these coastal profiles were an important comple-
ment to charts made during the voyage. (Museo Naval, Carpeta IV (87);
Higueras 2571)*

the easier name of Cabo Arcadio. This was at the entrance to Prince William Sound, and Suria recorded the difficulty in entering, passing between Montague and Magdalena Islands, the former to leeward and the latter to windward. They also "doubled another island [the Isla Triste of the Spanish accounts] that was in the middle of the channel and which cost us much trouble to pass on account of the force of the wind, which was from the bow."

A boat was readied and entrusted to Pilot José María Sánchez for inspection of the nearby coast seeking a place where the corvettes could with some security drop anchor in the interior of Port Santiago (Port Etches).[2] The violence of the wind, and of a particularly strong gust, both foiled the intent to enter and snapped the *Descubierta*'s yard arm of the topgallant at its base.

Suria ascribed the gusts to the blowing of wind through the openings in the mountains, and indicated that the *Descubierta*'s accident had caused some disorder and confusion. Realizing that entry into Prince William Sound was going to be very difficult if not impossible, Malaspina "resolved to sheer off and content himself with having reached the entrance of Príncipe Guillermo and thus having exceeded the order of the court which had commanded him to go up to 60° latitude. Here we were in 61° and some minutes, the season was advanced, and he [Malaspina] considered that we should prepare for our return to Acapulco."[3] The boat under Pilot Sánchez returned to the corvettes, was put aboard, and the vessels stood out to sea by tacking. This was their deepest penetration northward, and each league convinced them that there was not going to be any pass to the Atlantic in those northern latitudes. Just by observation from the ships during clear weather, the huge land masses and their escarpment down to the Pacific Ocean were all the testimony that was needed. A more thorough exploration of the coast from Cape Hinchinbrook to Cape Fairweather was indispensable, not only to dispel once and for all the doubts which might remain about the desired passage, but also because "this was a piece of the coast which, except for the great mountain of St. Elias,...is not known to have been seen by any traveler."[4] Furthermore, the season in those northerly latitudes was already very much advanced.

Tomás Suria became extremely patriotic at that moment and recorded his thoughts in his journal.

These justifiable considerations deprived us in part of the glory of following the route projected of going up to 70° or 80° where the Glacial Sea [Arctic Ocean] and the South Sea [Pacific Ocean] unite by the Bering Strait, and carry out the same explorations as the immortal Cook. This created the greatest desires of our commander and the officers of both corvettes to find ourselves in such a favourable position,...Between this coast and the last part of America is found the true and indicated Strait of Bering where ends this considerable part of the world. This is not traversable as these seas are constantly frozen, although various nations have entered it. Spain does not take second place to any nation in heroism as it has always shown during all the centuries, whenever she sends out subjects of known valour and prudence such as our actual commander [Malaspina]. On this occasion this was particularly noticeable, for even the humblest sailors formed bands which murmured about the plans taken of reconnoitring the coast because they were ignorant of the real motives, which with the accord of the officers, had been reached in the cabin. They believed that what was a wise precaution was a lack of spirit and their disgust and impatience were notable because they came to believe that the English had the advantage of us in these discoveries. Our commander, far from being disquieted by such demonstrations of the natural and inveterate spirit of heroism of our nation, gave as an example an invitation to a celebration in the cabin in view of the officers, thus prudently cutting short such rumours.[5]

Wolf's head helmet, Tlingit, late eighteenth century. (Museo de América 13.913)

Inclement weather resulted in an unanticipated stay near the entrance to Prince William Sound, during which time several islands and other prominent geographical features had earlier names confirmed on the maps or were given Spanish names. Some small islands called Hijosa were so named in honour of the Commissary of the Naval Department of San Blas, Francisco de Hijosa, and a large island was named for the absent Galiano, "for the senior grade lieutenant attached to this commission, for whom because of his talent and love of work there should be preserved in our memory a distinguished location."[6]

On the morning of 12 July the corvettes were approached by a skin canoe like those of Port Mulgrave. It contained two Indians "in their respective holes and with their arrows and lances tied on the deck of the canoe by way of precaution." The Spaniards repeatedly invited them to come aboard, but they could not be persuaded. Rather, they gave the well-known signs of friendship by stretching out their arms and repeating *La li, La li!,* the equivalent, according to Suria, of *koacan* or friend. They held aloft on a pole a prime sea otter pelt which seemed to the Spaniards the best that they had seen up to that time. With it, the natives hoped to convince the Spaniards to anchor in a port which, according to the signs they were making, lay on the west side of Hijosa Island. The Indians offered to serve as guides.

Suria indicated that: "The dress which the natives in Montague [Island, at the entrance to Prince William Sound] wear consists of sea otter skins, [and] a blouse of flexible and transparent gut, the folds of which are fastened around the hole in the canoe. Their hats are like Chinese hats, their hair is loose, covered with red ochre, their ears and nose are bored, and hanging from these are some long narrow leather thongs like tape, while passing through the nose is a tooth of bone of some land animal."[7]

Tova leaves a similar account of the approach on 15 July of a skin canoe with two natives who came out from Galiano Island. This was followed by the visit of a pirogue with fourteen persons, which native craft was able to keep up with the *Descubierta*, then making about four knots. "We reciprocated the signs of friendship and urged them to come aboard, offering all the merchandise that we thought might interest their curiosity or ambition; but to everything they answered by showing us some very fine sea otter pelts, which we could buy in great quantity if we anchored at their island." To Tova this reception was evident proof that other European vessels had anchored there or that they had commerce with the natives at Prince William Sound.[8]

In the ensuing days the coast was followed closely but not without difficulty. This gave Bauzá a chance to observe, measure and map Mount St. Elias. Suria drew several views of the coast, "one of them particularly exact, which the geographer [Bauzá] adopted for the collection."[9] Spanish place names were again bestowed, most of which did not have lasting application, and some of which were replacement names for previous non-Spanish toponyms. Most significant was the growing conviction that there was no strait to be found.

The crews were extremely tired from constant activity, so on the night of 24-25 July anchor was cast to give them needed rest. Despite the corvettes' eleven kilometre distance from shore, they saw a lone Indian who came out intending to pay a visit, but prior to arriving seemed to repent of his decision. However, Valdés, who was out in one of the boats, convinced the native to come aboard. After he tied his canoe to the stern, the native ascended to the quarterdeck and reissued an invitation to come to his village where he "offered us means to satisfy our desires." He presented a basket of strawberries

and traded his sea otter cape for little bells, a looking glass and beads, which he greatly esteemed, although he indicated he would have preferred hatchets. The Spaniards noted that his language was somewhat different from that of the inhabitants of Port Mulgrave, of whom he spoke as being valorous warriors. He also showed a knowledge of firearms, gained either from dealings with other Europeans or with the Mulgraves. Finally, at 8 P.M. he went off in his canoe "very happy with our attentions and offering to repeat the visit the following day."[10]

Malaspina commented on offers of prostitution by local Indians who tried to lure the corvettes to their village. He wrote: "Finally, their readiness to offer us the use of their women, with the same ease which had been offered to us so many times in Port Mulgrave, left us without doubt that we were not the first Europeans known by these natives."[11] Although Malaspina indicated that the only Europeans to anticipate his visit to Yakutat Bay were the British under Dixon, some minor bits of evidence suggest other contacts. Perhaps one of these was the rather distant contact at Lituya Bay where the Lapérouse expedition had visited.

Heading eastward, the explorers stayed close to shore and sighted en route three openings along the coast which they named Ensenada de Castilla, Entrada de Aragón and Bahía de Palma. At night, two lights were visible, one in the direction of Ensenada de la Cruz [Cross Sound], and the other toward Puerto de los Remedios, both giving indication of native habitation. During all this time Felipe Bauzá drew coastal views of most of these salient geographical features.

Early August brought an abrupt shift in the weather. Instead of the changeable but frequently contrary winds that had foiled some of the previous plans of exploration, the corvettes were surprised by a heavy

Snow-covered Mount St. Elias is a prominent feature on the Alaskan coast, mentioned in accounts left by early explorers and traders. Standing offshore are the Descubierta *(at left, flying the pennant of the commander)* *and the* Atrevida. *From a pencil and wash sketch attributed to Felipe Bauzá. (Museo de América 2-248; Palau 42, Sotos 554)*

fog, so thick that it was necessary to exchange cannon shot signals in order to stay together.[12] The fog prevented an intended visit to Bucareli Bay. There was also evident a great deal of seaweed and kelp, "a marine plant like an orange with a long stem, the leaves of which are somewhat like those of a vine. This plant keeps all of its foliage when underneath the water, but immediately withers when out of it. We collected some of it and found out by experiment what I have just set down. The botanist, Haenke, both described them and added them to his herbarium."[13]

The first days of August were accompanied by much wind and heavy seas, though not totally unmanageable. But on 5 August, the wind began to blow with hurricane force, the like of which the men had seldom experienced. According to Suria, Malaspina called it the worst he had seen in all the voyage from Cádiz, and was worried, though he tried to hide it. The artist was greatly impressed with the difficulties faced by the Spanish explorers and exaggerated them somewhat:

The signs previously referred to of a great number of whales and other fish swimming about, jumping and appearing on the surface, awakened our vigilance, leading us to expect every instant a strong storm, as these signs are usually sure ones. Actually the wind came up from the southeast so excessively strong that it was necessary to handle the ship with every care, furling the topgallant sails, the mainsail and the foretopsail and remaining only with the topsail and the foresail. The wind kept getting stronger every instant, with rain and a very heavy sea. The swells were tremendous and the darkness terrifying. This unfortunate event obliged us to stand off from the Isla Carlota [Queen Charlotte Islands, thought at the time to be one island] which bore eastsoutheast in order to run before the wind for safety. Thus we ran for six days of terrific storm. If it had not been for the wonderful construction of our vessels, built purposely to withstand every class of danger, we would without doubt have perished, as it seemed as if all the elements had conspired against us. There was not a man who could keep his footing, simply from the violence of the wind, so that besides the mountains of water and foam which swept over us, there arose from the surface of the water small drops of spray forming a strange and copious rainfall never before seen. The roaring noise of both elements was horrible and terrifying. The confusion and shouting on the ship, together with the maledictions of the sailors, who in such cases break out into blasphemy, augmented the terror to such an extent that it seemed as if all the machinery of the universe were ready to destroy us. During this time we suffered such inconveniences as cannot be described, for during the six days there was no one who could get repose for a moment.[14]

The storm, however magnified in Suria's journal, was sufficient to prevent the expedition from penetrating Dixon Entrance, and almost before they knew it the explorers found themselves not far from Nootka. In order to thank the sailors for the good work they had done and at the same time to prevent an outbreak of scurvy, the *Descubierta* crew was treated to lemonade on the advice of the ship's physician. The *Atrevida* followed suit. This refreshment was also given to the officers and others in the wardrooms of both vessels.[15]

Completion of the various northern explorations which resulted in the conviction that there was no strait to be found in the area both north and south of Mulgrave, brought consideration of the second of the important orders which had diverted the original intent of the round-the-world naval scientific exploring expedition and brought Malaspina to the Pacific Northwest Coast. The expedition was tasked to visit Nootka Sound and report on the small, exposed settlement that had clung to existence there for just over two years.

A Visit to Nootka

It was 10 August at 11 A.M. when the coast of Nootka was espied and shortly thereafter Tahsis Peak, which stood out on the horizon, was seen. "The first view of the coast indicated that it was low, because, although the mountains could be seen, they were not very high. Their lightness or darkness made manifest the different locations which they had above the level of the sea."[1]

As the corvettes closed on land, they were met by two Indian canoes, but unable to pull alongside, these went off. When the wind slackened, the corvettes lost the weigh they had on and were becalmed opposite Puerto de la Esperanza. At 3 P.M. two other canoes came out asking for Monterey abalone shells, the favourite trade item. Some Indians climbed aboard without the aid of a ladder and continued their quest for trade with the words *pachitle conchi*, give us shells. This phrase was accompanied by their saying *Hispania Nutka*, followed by words that meant alliance and friendship. "We were astonished to hear from their mouths Latin words such as Hispania," wrote Malaspina, "but we concluded that perhaps they had learned this word in their trading with Englishmen or that it was a bad pronunciation. They also asked for bread and other kinds of food, indicating to us that our flag, language and customs were not strange to them, nor were the names of our commanders Martínez and Eliza. They let us know that only one of our vessels was in port. After some time the native boats departed in order to return ashore."[2]

At 5 P.M., with the wind failing, the incoming vessels hoisted their insignias, hoping that the shore establishment might see them and learn of their proximity. "You can imagine the sensation that it was for us to see shortly afterward the national flag waving on a promontory next to the south point, and among the trees to make out the three masts of an unrigged vessel."[3]

At nightfall a longboat could be seen rounding the point to the eastnortheast which after two hours of hard rowing reached the incoming corvettes. It had aboard some twenty men and a coxswain who had been sent by the senior naval officer, Ensign Ramón Saavedra, to help in any way possible. It was already too late for any activity that day, so Malaspina ordered the boat and its crew to remain for the night.[4]

Santa Cruz de Nutka, as the settlement from which the longboat had come was called, was a token garrison established to protect and enhance Spanish claim to sovereignty over the coast north of the already occupied area of California. As a military post, it was situated at a point of easy access, having appropriated the site of the native village of Yuquot, but certainly in a location ill-suited for maintenance of any self-supporting operations. Besides need for continual outside aid, the location on an offshore island adjacent to Vancouver Island would never have supported Iberian-style agriculture nor have sufficient land to support a mission, an institution so essential to the Spanish northward advance.

Suria indicated in his journal that it was the desire of Malaspina to treat with the Nootka natives, in view of great things said about them by all travellers, both Spaniards and Englishmen, as well as his wish to clarify the nature of the area contiguous to the existing settlement. He also wanted to correct the foreign maps of the area because he considered them to be incorrect, in view of the little concordance of those charts with Spanish maps.[5]

On 11 August, the morning following their arrival offshore, the corvettes had little difficulty entering Nootka Sound. The Captain of the Catalonian Volunteer detachment, Don Pedro Alberni, as senior commander of the fort, rendered the proper salute, as did the Frigate *Concepción*, but this military courtesy was not reciprocated for fear of alteration of the marine chronometer movement. As had been the case the day before when the corvettes were still off the harbour entrance, a local supply of fresh vegetables and fish were sent aboard. Soon both Alberni and Saavedra presented themselves aboard, where Malaspina served them a good breakfast.[6]

Finally, these ceremonies completed, the corvettes were made secure with anchors and cables. Suria recorded: "The port is not the most capacious and the entrance... is very narrow. Two small vessels can scarcely sail out or enter it together. It makes a figure similar to this [Suria added a rough sketch to his journal], aside from the many islands and farallones which are close to the coast." The anchoring ground was so limited that the three corvettes were almost moored together.[7]

Malaspina early learned from acting commandant Saavedra that his superior, Lieutenant Francisco de Eliza, had left Nootka at the beginning of May to continue northward exploration to Puerto Bucareli and the Dixon Strait Passage, but actually spent most of his time in an exploration of the Strait of Juan de Fuca and the southern portions of the Strait of Georgia. Eliza took the Brig *San Carlos* as his flag ship and the tiny schooner *Saturna* [short for *Santa Saturnina*] as his companion vessel for exploration of shallow areas. The schooner was the product of Spanish shipbuilding on the Northwest Coast, being one of the many activities in which the members of the garrison had been involved, in addition to eking out an existence. Eliza was at that time expected to return from his reconnaissance via the Bahía de Buena Esperanza, making an interior loop around most of Mazarredo Island, as the Spanish called Nootka Island,[8] in his return to his home port at Santa Cruz de Nutka. His return occurred just two days after

Friendly Cove in Nootka Sound as it appeared in the summer of 1791 when visited by Malaspina. The observatory can be seen on the shore behind the depot guard ship, the Concepción. *The battery of San Miguel, constructed by Martínez in 1789, commands the entrance to the small bay. Ink and wash drawing by José Cardero. (Museo de América 2.270; Palau 66, Sotos 593)*

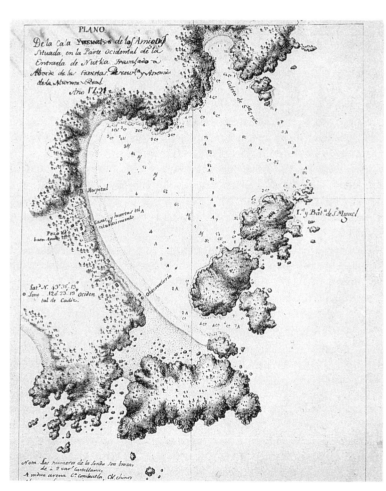

This plan of Friendly Cove was later engraved for the 1802 publication of the journal of the 1792 voyage. (Museo Naval Sig. II D-17; Higueras 2069)

Tadeo Haenke was experienced in mathematics, astronomy, medicine and botany. An accomplished musician and linguist, he made a major contribution to the scientific achievements of the voyage. (Courtesy Josef Kuhnel)

departure of the *Descubierta* and *Atrevida*, thereby depriving the naval scientists of knowledge of an area of considerable concern to them. What might have happened if Malaspina had delayed several days, or if Eliza had not been delayed by adverse winds in his return to Nootka? Would Malaspina have altered his plans and entered the Strait of Juan de Fuca? Would he have discovered Puget Sound or the Inland Passage? Or would he have detached some of his men to make such a reconnaissance in one of the vessels potentially available? Or would he have done just what he did, that is, return to Acapulco?

Additional news gained upon entry into the Cala de los Amigos as the Spaniards called Friendly Cove, was that Lieutenant Jacinto Caamaño had earlier left for San Blas in the Corvette *Princesa* with forty ill persons, many of them with scurvy and at great risk, for which reason he had proposed to stop off at Monterey to seek fresh supplies for their relief. Finally, it was indicated that the Frigate *Aránzazu* had left for Monterey where it expected to take aboard for delivery to Nootka a supply of meat and fresh provisions and other most urgent needs.[9]

From the very moment of his arrival, Malaspina's work was facilitated by the helpfulness of Saavedra, who told the visitors all that he knew about the country. This was followed by an even more informed source, Pedro Alberni, "the distinguished official who," wrote Suria, "will occupy one of the most worthy places in the account of this voyage as a result of his skill and management of these natives, and who was charged with sustaining the establishment and keeping it free from invasions."[10]

Routine activity while in port went on without any difficulty, beginning the very first day. Customary temperature readings were taken morning, noon and night, with the following initial results of 57, 60.2 and 59.8 degrees Fahrenheit, with a fresh wind from the southwest and very clear skies and horizon. The observatory tent was taken ashore and set up, and next to it a shed was made to house both the pendulums and the barometer. The masts were inspected, repaired and treated. The astronomers began taking observations, while the sailors spent time repairing some cables and constructing a mast for the longboat, a replacement for one broken earlier. The botanist, Don Tadeo Haenke, began to botanize. He made a collection of plants, but very meagre because he could not find in port other plants distinct from those of Europe. However, he did find many anti-scorbutic plants, classifying these, as well as the pines of which there were many different species. One document resulted: a "Notice of some of the plants which are found in the vicinity of the Port of Santa Cruz de Nutka, classified by the Botanist Don Luis Née."[11] It seems strange that Née, who was not present and was clearly less competent than Haenke, would be given credit for such a listing.

Similar to the effort made while at Yakutat in early July, the Malaspina stay at Nootka resulted in a short list of useful timber to be found there. Naval construction potential was again emphasized.

Timber of the Port of Nootka
For masts and yards of all vessels.
1. Pine with very thin smooth white bark and .6 cm thick. It has few knots and the largest ones are 3.2 cm in diameter and it was from this tree that a mast was made. It is light, flexible, and it gives off an aromatic white pitch.
2. Fir tree. It has a dark and somewhat rough bark which is not very thick. It has some knots but not very large. It has little sapwood. It is light, flexible and somewhat streaked and gives off pitch the colour of egg yolk. From this tree a topmast was made.
3. Pine of a thick black bark with white streaks, very rough and with

many large knots. It has much sapwood and is heavy. It is good for heavy planks and canoes because it is thicker than the other kinds. Its branches can be used for knees and seizing, and for charcoal.

4. Easily split pine. It has not very thick, rough, dark-coloured bark. The leaf is wider than that of the rest and of it a beer is made. It is very fissile. It gives off much pitch which the natives make use of for their wounds. At the end it has many knots. It is good for planking and from its roots various futtocks and knees can be made for vessels up to 200 tons.

5. Cypress pine. It has dark, thick bark and the natives make use of it to manufacture their clothing and ropes. It is weak wood and fissile, but very light. From it the natives make planks by splitting it with wedges along the grain of the tree, and they press them to make them straight.

Under these trees is found in abundance a type of short grass that is found in these high latitudes which they call moss. It grows in the shade and on the rocks. With this they caulk the clinker-built vessels in Galicia. After it is dry, it is placed between various boards and once it enters the water it expands so as to make it as tight as if done with oakum and of greater duration. They also weave with it.[12]

Besides the regular observations, Suria tells us, there was time for the crews to make a casual inspection of their new surroundings:

Every afternoon for a respite from our labours, we went to walk on the beaches. These are composed of small stones of various kinds of marble and jasper, the greater part black, as on all the coast. They were in spherical and elliptical form, very pleasing, and for curiosity's sake all of them were collected. The forest close to the beaches is extremely thick. Nature is here observed in its rustic and rare state. It is necessary to travel through it with much care, as, during the course of years and the fact that the natives do not cultivate it, trees have been accumulating on top of each other.[13]

Both on 14 August under Lieutenant Francisco de Viana and on 15 August led by Secundino Salamanca, the launches of both vessels went out for reprovisioning of water. As much other shipboard work as conveniently possible was shifted to the beach where blacksmiths and carpenters could work with more ample space. For making a better local map, Bauzá and one of the apprentice pilots, Juan Inciarte, went to set up landmarks on several of the nearby islands and to lay out a baseline at Resolution Cove, the anchorage that Captain Cook had used while at Nootka.[14]

Malaspina's party made a detailed evaluation of the progress of agricultural experiments which had been carried out at Nootka. Leader in these efforts was Pedro Alberni, commanding officer of garrison troops, whose efforts won a great deal of admiration from the round-the-world explorers.[15] The limited suitable area ashore was very quickly planted "in gardens from which were picked vegetables of exquisite taste, most useful refreshment not only for sailors who arrive at that port after long and weary voyages, but also for individuals employed in the establishment itself, among whom previously scurvy had made great inroads." By availing himself of those who "before taking up the gun, had handled the plow," and by putting them to work at cultivation of plants, Alberni managed to change "thick brambles into an agreeable and useful stopping place for the mariner." The Malaspina group was much interested in the horticultural efforts being carried out at Nootka and recorded the following:

Notice of the crops that are grown at Nootka.
Cabbage, garlic and onions are grown in summer and are conserved in winter without bloating or shrinkage. The largest cabbages are over 4 to 5 kilograms; the onions and garlic are produced with the same abundance

as in Europe. Lettuce, chard, radishes, turnips, carrots, parsley and artichokes are produced all summer long until the month of November.

Both lettuce and radishes reached gargantuan proportions. The latter were described by the visitors as being as large as a person's thigh, and always tender, while the lettuce was said to be three times as large as normal. In the line of less phenomenal productivity, the garrison gardens produced all types of squash, but very small. Tomatoes, too, were small and did not mature well. "Beans and peas are also produced with abundance, but in rainy years they become soft, so that normally they can only be used green. Chickpeas produce large vines but do not granulate."

According to a report by Bustamante, wheat and corn met the same fate as chickpeas. Attempts to sow these two useful grains at one-week intervals during the early part of the year in order to find the proper time for planting, all resulted in the same failure. Barley showed some promise, maturing well and yielding about 12 or 14 to 1.

Alberni's potatoes thrived. However, it was noted that all crops needed great care in order to produce, because either the excess of rain rotted them or the lack of rain made them subject to worms. In support of these agricultural efforts some enlisted men were assigned to full time duty as gardeners.

In other efforts aimed at self-sufficiency, Alberni turned his talents to propagation of domestic fowls. He raised turkeys, chickens and ducks. The count at the time of Malaspina's visit in 1791 reached 60 hens and 400 chicks, to which was added the note that the hens laid eggs all year long despite the frequent cold and rain. Alberni's poultry production was reported to "have cost him much inconvenience because despite the diligence with which they have been pursued, the rats which had been brought with the vessels spread with even greater rapidity." In fact, they had burrowed the entire area of the Spanish establishment and were consuming the supplies stored in the warehouses, as well as damaging the sails of the ships that were stored in the same warehouses. Modest efforts at livestock production at the small Nootka garrison were also reported as of August 1791 as follows: two (or in some reports four) cows, one bull, one she-goat, one ewe and twenty pigs, both male and female. The pigs were kept on an island between the mainland and the garrison, known as Isla de los Cerdos, translated later as Hog Island, and today site of the lighthouse. Attempts to keep these animals under restraint, rather than allow them to wander into the interior of Nootka Island, motivated this use of a natural corral.

Nearer the inhabited nucleus, gardens were laid out and tended with care. Contemporary maps indicate which parcels had been set aside for the senior naval commander and for the army officer in charge of the garrison. Part of the success in agriculture was attributed to the fact that the Spaniards had the advantage of human fertilizer, since the land involved had been the settlement area of the Nootkans[16] prior to arrival of the Spaniards. The scientific visitors ate native foods, such as blackberries, and Alberni seems to have introduced domesticated varieties as well. Even today, local native tradition distinguishes between the indigenous, wild blackberries and those brought during the Spanish period.

Malaspina recognized that continual activity on the part of those stationed at Nootka produced benefits in both health and morale. He commented that Francisco de Eliza and Pedro Alberni "realized immediately that the fitness of these people depended more on continual activity than on the medicines with which they could be helped.

Clearing away the forest toward the ocean and toward the establishment was the first useful attempt at such tasks, after which there followed very shortly the construction of a schooner [the *Santa Saturnina*], and the beginning of various buildings destined either for workshops, or quarters, or storage of supplies." He asserted that if the "vegetables had not taken hold so quickly, circumstances would have been disagreeable and possibly fatal; but the facility with which cabbage, lettuce, onions, garlic, chard, radishes, turnips, carrots, parsley and artichokes began to take on vigour certainly not only led many more [persons] to the useful occupation of cultivation, but also placed a great obstacle to the relentless inroads of scurvy."

The naval scientist, filled with optimism, indicated that "at the same time they were able to make new experiments with seeds. Although the garbanzos, wheat and corn did not live up to expectations, barley and potatoes certainly did, and the beans and peas, provided the rains are not excessive, gave evidence that a comfortable existence of a colony on this coast would no longer be precarious and dependent on either hunting or fishing."[17]

The agricultural efforts were viewed somewhat less enthusiastically by Geographer Felipe Bauzá, though he admitted the successes of the gardens planted and cared for by Alberni. But "they only have four cows, a bull and a few goats; and they cannot hope greatly to be able to keep much livestock because of the narrowness of the land and the lack of pasturage in winter. It is difficult to harvest sufficient wheat and corn for the maintenance of the Indians of the settlement due to the limited amount of land and the difficulty of cutting back the forest, since everything is surrounded by very large trees, and although they fell them with the aid of fire, carrying them off from that location by any means whatsoever is very difficult and slow, while the combination of rain, together with the problem of [limited] sunshine, are obstacles which impede making such useful harvests."[18]

Concerning deployment of the Nootka garrison, Malaspina obtained from Ramón Saavedra, commanding officer of the *Concepción*, a list of the activities in which the crew of that frigate was daily employed. This report indicated that there were 13 employed as wood cutters and carriers of wood and water. Six men were in charge of food and livestock, while two men, Artilleryman José Quintana and Sailor Pedro José Peres [*sic*], were tending the gardens. One bricklayer, Salvador Rivera, was employed in his specialty, and seven men were assigned to the bakery.[19] All who resided at the precarious Spanish settlement at Nootka exerted great efforts to make the area livable for a group of displaced Hispanics, and despite the successes that the garrison had in some fields, the Malaspina expedition members appreciated the difficulty of the job assigned to the local residents. Illness had depleted their ranks, with the death of some of the garrison whose last resting place was the spot of land where Meares had established his short-lived post at the Ensenada de los Muertos (Dead Men's Cove), and with the return of others to more salubrious southern climes. The ailments most common at the Nootka establishment were "colds, colics, rheumatic pains, scurvy, and diarrhea or bloody dysentery, the latter two being most common and almost incurable." Many of those most affected had departed before the arrival of the corvettes, having been evacuated, as mentioned, aboard the Frigate *Princesa*. As a result of their departure, the Nootka garrison was shorthanded of both men and officers.

Shortage of able-bodied personnel was also a problem for the Malaspina expedition. One incident at Nootka illustrates the attrition brought on by the arduous life at sea. John Green, an artilleryman aboard the *Atrevida*, had signed aboard at the outset of the voyage while the vessel was still in Cádiz. He was of New England Presbyterian background but had before enlistment "abjured the errors of the Presbyterian sect," of which act the chaplain of the *Atrevida* had official certification. How the Bostonian had arrived in Spain, as well as his motivation for enlistment, are unknown. While in Acapulco, Green had become ill of what was reported as dropsy, though this may not have been a very precise diagnosis of his condition. He had concealed his malady for fear that if he had disclosed it, he would have been left behind in that unhealthful climate until completion of the projected visit to the Northwest Coast.

As time passed in northern latitudes, Green's condition slowly worsened, the result of northern fogs, winds and long hours of navigation. While at Nootka, on the morning of 26 August 1791, the suffering mariner at "his urgent request" was given the last rites, with Father Chaplain Francisco de Paula Aniño administering the sacraments of Penance, the Holy Eucharist and Extreme Unction. The Mass celebrated for him at that time was apparently one with military honours, for all the men were in formation. Perhaps the most impressed spectator was the young Nootka chief Keischconuc [Keiskonuk], "who showed great satisfaction in seeing the troops under arms, but demonstrating at the same time his fear, which he was not able to overcome completely, and after a while he found it necessary to retire."[20] For eighteen more days, John Green held on, until shortly after the expedition arrived in Monterey where he died and was buried in the presidio chapel.[21]

The few Franciscan priests who were sent to Nootka were there as chaplains rather than as missionaries, with evidence of their activities in proselytizing almost completely absent. Nootka tradition suggests that the Catholic priests played a significant role, and this is buttressed by the fact that there is a deteriorating Catholic church at Friendly Cove, with a stained glass window depicting Franciscan Father Magín Catalá, a much later addition commemorating the ancient Spanish presence there. There is no evidence of that native of Montblanch, Catalonia, having acted as a missionary there, but he did serve as chaplain aboard the *Aránzazu* in the area during 1792, 1793 and 1794. Although Christianization of the local Indians was not a high priority, and seems to have received limited attention, control of native friendship and support by the local Indians was essential to the continued presence of the small colony consisting of seamen from the Naval Department of San Blas and a few soldiers, principally from the Second Company of the Voluntarios de Cataluña, the famous Catalonian Volunteers of Borderlands history.

Communication with the natives was not as difficult at Nootka since there had been prior visitors who already knew the language, giving opportunity for checking words against established usage. Furthermore, at Nootka one of the enlisted men stationed there, corporal of dragoons Gabriel del Castillo of Guadalajara, had special duty and increased pay as a Nootka interpreter, though there is reason to believe that his capacity was not as great as the credit that he was given for such ability. The basis for his special linguistic skill is not known, but some competence is attested to by one fact – he was not permitted to return home to Mexico as scheduled because his presence was "indispensable." This feeling of great utility was not shared by Malaspina group members who had occasion to use his services. They asserted that he knew very little Nootkan.

A limited number of Nootkan words was added to the longer list of Tlingit words from Mulgrave:

hyitjo	=	knife
natchesuchek	=	mirror
Alape	=	[a Nootka subordinate chief]
Caliquin	=	the one killed by Martínez
Nasape	=	brother of Maquina
as	=	many
choco a co	=	come here
Guasg	=	glass
Guancomo (with a strong "g")	=	wooden mask
Matuate	=	bird
Chiapus	=	hat
Nitchitle	=	to sew.[22]

Diplomacy on the Northwest Coast

At the time of Malaspina's arrival at Yuquot, Spanish-Indian relations had reached their lowest point. Early Spanish dealings with the Nootkans, and particularly with their chief, Maquinna,[23] had been exceptionally good, in large measure because the Spaniards came well equipped with trade goods and presents calculated to impress the Nootkans and had used these judiciously. Some of the specific items which were taken aboard for trade with native people were enumerated in a listing of stores aboard the *Atrevida*. These included a supply of knives, scissors, crude razors, packages of jet, glass and false coral beads and some little mirrors.[24] The Spaniards cared very little for reciprocal gifts except for items needed to gratify their scientific curiosity and to become personal souvenirs, such as artifacts of native manufacture. Since they planned no additional stops other than a re-

cuperation visit to Monterey in California and then return to Mexico, the Malaspina party could be generous in gift giving and even prodigal in providing what by Nootka standards were lavish banquets. It is no wonder that the memory of Malaspina's visit lingered long in the minds of many Nootkans, particularly the chiefs.

For Malaspina it was not sufficient merely to be friends with Maquinna. He had to make positive strides to overcome the great misgivings of that Nootka chieftain which had resulted in the existing estrangement. Callicum's death, for which Spanish officer Estevan José Martínez, the pilot commanding the Frigate *Princesa*, had been responsible, was much too vivid in the collective Indian memory. Renewal of friendship was tied to a second Spanish purpose which had become Malaspina's responsibility. The mariner was there to reassure himself, for later reporting to the court, that the Spanish pretensions concerning Nootka were truly as the diplomats were representing them to be in the negotiations going on between Spain and Great Britain.

Malaspina needed local evidence that British Captain John Meares had not at an early time purchased a specific tract of land from Maquinna, but that the Spaniards themselves had made a valid acquisition of the area with the consent of that sovereign. To do so it was necessary to strengthen local native feeling in favour of Spain and, therefore, against Great Britain. In addition to these political considerations, the Malaspina group viewed Maquinna as an ideal informant for the anthropological aspects of their studies. Who would be in a position to tell more about Nootka culture than the principal chief himself? In the coming days, Maquinna was a welcome guest aboard the corvettes. He is mentioned by name in the guard books on six different days after his initial visit, and on two occasions he became the subject of portraiture. As a result, he became recipient of copious gifts.

It was not Maquinna alone who was of interest to the visitors, for the subordinate chief Tlupananulg (spelled various ways) had even closer and earlier association with the Spanish explorers. Natzape, identified as a chief of the Nuchimases (Kwakiutl), was likewise recipient of gifts and was a subject of interest. Both of these important Pacific Northwest Coast subordinate chiefs had their portraits drawn by artist Tomás Suria, the former on 23 August and the latter on 27 August, both drawn wearing a typical basketry hat.

Chief Tlupananulg was the first of the Nootka leaders to make contact when he visited the *Atrevida* on 13 August at about 10 A.M., at which time he was identified as "third chief of this tribe and related to Taquina [*sic*], the principal chief."[25] At that time "we saw rounding the point inside the port which closes it and divides it from the channel which leads to the settlements of the chiefs, a large canoe of different shape from the ordinary ones. It was manned by ten rowers on a side and in the middle was the chief named Tlupanamibo [Tlupananulg] with a large square chest." He came aboard, confident and happy, all by himself. Through Captain Alberni and a Guadalajara boy, Castillo of the Frigate *Santa Gertrudis*, who served as interpreters, the mariners made out his harangue:

Great chief, Tlupanamibo, *tasi* (inferior) to you, has heard your polite and friendly message and in compliance with it and with the friendship which I profess for your nation and the great chief which directs you to our habitations, I have come to see you and salute you. I am convinced that you will be informed by Captain Alberni of the fidelity of my actions. He has experienced from me, and from my men by my command, better actions than words. He is here and can tell you the truth. I begin with this

discourse in order to gain your full confidence, the same that I expect that you will have in me.

Do not believe that my years can serve as an obstacle to serve you in what you may be pleased to order me to do. Although you may marvel and believe me a barbarian, I am not ignorant of the inviolable laws of friendship. They inspire me to tell you not to confide in nor feel safe from the dissimulated perfidy of Macuina. I tell you that he is crafty and overbearing and he looks on you with hatred and abhorrence. He shortly meditates dislodging you from this place which you have founded in our dominion, but he cannot do it while Tlupanamibo lives, who, being experienced in this double-crossing game, will know how to oppose it as I have his malign projects to the present.

Although, since I am his subject, I could accompany him in his enterprises, I forbear to do it because my heart is filled with integrity and justice. I know that you are men like us, but more civilized and united to the universal and particular interest of yourselves and of your nation, on which account I do not admire your manufactures and productions so much esteemed amongst us. The commoners do not yet think and so they attribute to prodigies and enchantments those operations you perform for the management of your great canoes. Finally, if you wish to gain the entire confidence of all the tribe, proceed as the English do, who although greedier, are upright and unchangeable and their treatment of us is familiar and gracious.[26]

Suria claimed that he was not taken in by Tlupananulg's rhetoric. "This elegant speech was so beautiful that our officers formed an elevated concept of this tribe, but I do not admire it as I recall the elegant way in which the Mexicans know how to deliver a harangue."[27]

During the Malaspina visit, this chief who had his village near the head of Tlupana Arm was a frequent visitor to the corvettes. He and his great war canoe, as well as his men, were subjects of various drawings done by the expedition artists in the following days. Al-

Maquinna, the dominant chief at Nootka, played a central role in negotiations with European visitors. Pencil drawing by Tomás de Suria. (Museo Naval, Carpeta I-27; Higueras 2936, Sotos 599)

Natzape, a secondary chief to Maquinna, provided the expedition's scientists with many details of local native customs. (Museo de América 2.264; Palau 60, Sotos 602)

Tlupananulg, another secondary chief, was instrumental in persuading a reluctant Maquinna to meet with Malaspina. Pencil and charcoal portrait by Tomás de Suria. (Museo Naval, Carpeta I (47); Higueras 2937, Sotos 598)

though Suria claimed to have been unimpressed by the unsolicited monologue of Tlupananulg, the artist's pencil and brush give the opposite impression.

It was not at the anchorage at Friendly Cove, nor was it Malaspina who tried to make the expedition's first contact with the reluctant Chief Maquinna. Rather it was a detached exploratory party under Valdés and Felipe Bauzá that attempted a first meeting with the Nootka chief, and this during a geodetic survey that they ran into the interior canals in the vicinity of Nootka and up Tahsis Canal.

It was already known that Maquinna was afraid of contact with the corvettes. His people in visits to the *Descubierta* and *Atrevida* had spoken of the extent of Maquinna's domains and of the solidity of his authority. However, on other occasions they let it be known that under different pretexts and excuses their chief was afraid to visit the Spaniards. This fear was specifically confirmed on 15 August when the two officers found the houses of Maquinna's interior village of Tahsis deserted. The local Indians had hidden themselves in the nearby forest and the Spaniards, though few in number, were scarcely able to get near any of the many Nootka Indians that they saw that day.

The stalemate was broken by another detachment from Malaspina's party under command of Lieutenants Cevallos and Espinosa which made a second trip to Tahsis and contacted the Nootka chief. This trip had been delayed by the need to complete the fabrication of a new mast for one of the launches, and had as one goal the extension of geodetic investigation as far as possible into the interior channels during a eight-day period that had been fixed for such activity.

Command was given to the two recently arrived officers, both of whom had travelled from Spain via Veracruz and Mexico City to join the exploring expedition shortly before its departure for the Pacific Northwest. They were selected for the reconnaissance so they might share in the glories that the other officers had already achieved, but of which they had thus far been deprived. Special preparations were made by mounting on the launches two swivel guns to be used in case of attack.

At the last moment before departure for the interior, Artist Suria had begged the commander to distinguish him by appointing him to "such a glorious small expedition." His request was granted and Malaspina provided him with a gun, pistols and ammunition as if he were a soldier, adding the necessary instruments for the operation of the business that he was to undertake. The artist left an interesting, if possibly exaggerated, account of the genesis of this small expedition, indicating that the instructions for it were to be opened at the foot of distant Mount Tahsis, an impossibility since time was limited and the peak would have been the area of deepest potential penetration, rather than a starting point. He also indicated that departure took place at 11:15 P.M. on 17 August at which time "with shouts and acclamations, we departed from the corvettes and commenced by rowing because there was a calm."[28] Orders were given particularly to see that these officers explored with sufficient care as to ascertain whether or not these channels had connection with the sea, and to be careful not to offend the natives nor to be surprised by them.

Malaspina's orders give in detail the operation that was contemplated:

Mr. Josef Espinosa:
    The task of the launches placed in your charge and that of Lieutenant Ciriaco Cevallos is to explore the arm of the sea east of the Port or Gulf of Nootka to learn if it reaches the sea in lower latitudes; if it is easy to navigate; and if it has in it products or people providing some incentive to visit it frequently. The launches are going out armed and provisioned for nine days and it has been arranged that you carry aboard them two soldiers from the shore garrison and a boatswain of the naval frigate [*Concepción*] for the purpose of serving as interpreters and as pilots, learning at the same time for the future everything that is suitable for the royal service and for this settlement. The following provisions, in addition to what your zeal and knowledge suggest, will serve for the most complete fulfillment of the indicated mission:

1) By carrying out the departure on the morning of the 18th, the return of the launches to this port will be precisely on the 25th at any time, so that for no reason that can be prevented can this expedition exceed the eight-day limit.

2) Navigation of the launches during this time must be directed to the arm to the right which has the greater appearance of penetration inland, and among the subdivisions or secondary channels those that lead toward the second quadrant [90° – 180°] or rather toward the south to join the ocean most rapidly are to be preferred for exploration.

3) Since in this excursion the greatest extent of exploration is to be preferred to a scrupulous hydrographic accuracy, it will be sufficient to establish a limit to the extremities with a couple of observations of latitude and longitude. By noting the turns of the channels and the time of sailing, it will be easy to obtain a more than average exactness in the work, taking advantage at the same time of the winds and tides that may be favourable. Sounding on these occasions will be more important than specific courses.

4) Maintenance of the boats and especially of the men in this commission will be viewed as of much greater importance than any exploration. They should be given normal daily rest and two or three hot meals; and oars will be used with moderation. They will be afforded the possibility of gathering vegetables, fish and meat, and if the weather becomes rainy with an east wind, and the coast becomes overcast, it is better to advance the return date than to expose the men to the least discomfort.

96

This portrait of "chiefs of Nootka" may depict Maquinna with one of his wives. Ink drawing by José Cardero. (Museo de América 2-266; Palau 62, Sotos 609)

5) As for everything concerning self-preservation and friendly contact with the natives, all possible precautions should be taken. The launches are never to be left beached; all arms are to be loaded when there are natives nearby; and the sentinels are to pass the word frequently for the purpose of avoiding any idea of surprise. You will use everything that you take with you in the launches to give presents if it seems opportune; and provided that neither self-preservation nor true national honour is compromised, you will avoid the least hostility.

6) If in any of the channels that you penetrate toward the sea you find foreign vessels, not only will you not feel yourselves charged with making evident the least national right, but rather you will try to make them understand immediately the objects of our expedition, or tasks, for all nations, and the utility of passing on to us any hydrographic information.

7) In places where it seems opportune, you will leave some coins buried and in a bottle news of the exploration with the date on which it was carried out. These will be the only evidences of our possession and they will be noted in the log, as well as everything that occurs on this trip.

8) You will bear in mind at the same time how important the physical reconnaissance of the coast that we frequent is to us, and thus you will not fail to gather specimens of everything belonging to the three kingdoms of natural history, examining particularly those products that may contribute to the prosperity of the settlement [of Nootka].[29]

Malaspina next wrote to his colleague, Bustamante, asking him to prepare the *Atrevida*'s launch to go out under Cevallos with nine days' rations, including a *cuartillo* (pint) of wine a day for each person. Its crew was to include Pilot Inciarte; a caulker, second class; and a marine. Also requested were munitions, rations for the interpreter and navigational instruments. The latter consisted of a Ramsden quarter-circle, and the #351 marine chronometer needed for taking required observations.[30] The extreme Spanish caution concerning encounters with the natives evoked suspicion in the native ranch-

View of a men's dance on the beach at Friendly Cove. It was the custom for visitors to circle the bay in their canoes three times upon arriving, singing a song proclaiming their identity and purpose. Tents on the beach are the observatory encampment set up by Malaspina's men. Ink and wash drawing by Tomás de Suria. (Museo Naval MS 1723-7; Higueras 2934, Sotos 596)

erias[31] visited during at least the early part of the exploration.[32] The officers in charge said that they were at first received with a disagreeable commotion. They saw the women and children retire, and various men approached them with clubs, heedless of the protestations of peace which the Spaniards offered to them.[33]

Upon departure from Friendly Cove, the two launches crossed Nootka Entrance and made a first stop at Resolution Cove to check the landmarks recently placed there. Subsequently, they continued on to the first long inlet to the right, Muchalat Arm. Next they inspected Tlupana Arm, always trending northward, but also exploring each inlet in accordance with their instructions.

The native inhabitants, located at the end of each canal, fled from their houses upon the approach of the launches, and even the chief himself, Tlupananulg, was so surprised in seeing such a show of force in that place that he could not help but ask the reason the launches were there. "It would have been impossible to give him the least idea of its commission," recorded Tova, "because the interpreters can only merit such a name for everyday things. But some gifts, accompanied by expressions of friendship and benevolence, convinced him better than if he had been shown the Ramsden quarter-circle and the Arnold longitude chronometer." He was mollified, so much so that he offered to accompany the Spanish officers in person everywhere, although as soon as he learned that they were going to Tahsis, he sought a pretext to separate.

On this occasion an easy out was provided for him by a letter which he delivered the following day at Friendly Cove. For this service which brought the expedition high command up to date, as well as for others which he had rendered to the establishment, he was given various presents and "was offered satisfaction of his desire for a sail for his great canoe, provided that with it he would carry out in our sight the manoeuvres that he had indicated."[34]

The Espinosa-Cevallos reconnaissance party continued its detailed exploration of the various arms, finally arriving at its important destination, even though the Spaniards already knew from native informants that the arm that they were exploring, Tahsis Canal, did not have any other outlet to the ocean, and that it was thus otherwise unnecessary to visit there except for their special instructions.

When they finally reached Maquinna's home village at Tahsis at the end of the long inlet of the same name, an even greater number of natives, armed for combat, greeted the small boat crews. At about 5 P.M. the two launches had approached the village of Maquinna's residence. They had by that time already determined that this arm of the sea terminated, as had all the others previously explored, in a great bay, but the explorers wanted to see the principal village. "The bad opinion of this chief, ... and the terror with which the natives fled from us the preceding days, were that many more reasons why we had to add great care to our conduct." Navigating their launches side by side, the Spaniards rowed toward Maquinna's village, where there now appeared a crowd of natives with arms in hand to prevent any landing.

The approaching visitors kept their arms hidden, but the Nootkans used theirs not for offensive operations, but in an effort to signal by gunshot to their fellow countrymen who were occupied elsewhere in routine tasks. When the Spaniards were within hailing distance, by means of an interpreter they informed the natives of the peaceful intent of the visit, and of the fact that they wanted to see and become acquainted with Maquinna, planning to use the services of a soldier of the Catalonian Volunteer company and a coxswain from the frigate *Concepción*, the local station vessel, as interpreters.

Despite this Spanish interest, Maquinna delayed for more than fifteen minutes "in showing his august person." The visiting party said in its report:

We did not spare any sign which might express our respect for such a high personage: We begged him to come aboard, and thinking to stimulate his cupidity, we showed him all those things which could be attractive to an inhabitant of Nootka; but the proud chief went away without answering a word, and after having cast upon us any number of glances filled with indifference.[35]

Undaunted, Espinosa and Cevallos were fortified in their desire to visit Maquinna in his own house. The lieutenants got out of their launches and, by means of a small boat or canoe, went ashore, leaving Pilot Inciarte in charge of the larger craft. The launches were sent off a respectable distance from the shore to prevent any disorder on the part of the sailors, while the officers, accompanied by only an interpreter, went ashore.

This demonstration of confidence changed Maquinna's attitude from one of a mixture of coldness, anger and fear, to that of genial host. The multitude of local Indians withdrew at the time of the arrival of the two naval officers, and Maquinna reciprocated the confidence displayed by Espinosa and Cevallos. The chief met the two Spaniards halfway between his long house and the landing place with an air of affability which in no way accorded with his previous conduct. Shortly thereafter, surrounded by local Nootkans who had reassembled, the Spaniards were ushered by Maquinna into his home. The first thing they noticed was his armoury of fourteen muskets, all in good condition, and a man with another musket acting as sentinel and

assuming the manual of arms position of "parade rest," by leaning on his musket. It appeared that the native guard was attempting to imitate his Spanish counterparts at the garrison at Yuquot. This armoury and this sentinel gave as much pride and superiority to Maquinna over the other chiefs, "as he was filled by vanity with the adornment of four windows which the American [John] Kendrik [*sic*] had installed for him, making him pay for it at a good price."

Maquinna next introduced his favourite wife, "whose attractive figure did not surprise us any less than the sentinel and the muskets." Three other wives were also presented, but the first was outstanding for her "beautiful features, smooth skin, and vivacity." She was a young girl of 20 or 21 years of age, sister of the well-liked subordinate chief Natzape. Amidst the other Nootka women, this wife was particularly notable for her very white skin and the delicacy of her features. The only qualification of the Spaniards' judgement was that perhaps they had been at sea too long: "If after a lengthy voyage one could judge beauty with accuracy, we would dare say that this vivacious girl exceeds in beauty the heroines of the novel, as they are pictured to us by the magic of poetry and by the creative imagination of poets."

After having distributed some presents, Cevallos wanted to please the favourite wife by showing her a picture that he had of his wife, whose likeness he carried in a little box. Maquinna looked at it first, then passed it to his preferred wife, who, after looking at it for some time with the greatest attention, praised the beauty of the lieutenant's wife. The visitors thought, however, that she contemplated it with that "attention that women usually give to those whom they consider to be rivals of theirs and can challenge them for the beauty prize." To the visitors, her face and actions "indicated that Nootka women were not free either from envy, when they find themselves inferior in personal merit to other women."

Espinosa and Cevallos recognized in Maquinna at this time a "mixture of great love and consideration toward his wife and at the same time a not inconsiderable amount of jealousy, although [according to their admission] at that moment they did not fail to notice the agreeable surprise of beauty that was as perfect as it was unexpected." Maquinna was not one to hide his feelings of jealousy, for when the officers insisted that he reestablish his headquarters at Yuquot close to the Spanish settlement, the Nootka chief answered that were he to do so, right away the Spaniards would try to violate the connubial rights of his Indians. Maquinna admitted that the "Spanish Chiefs," by their example and their punishments, tried to restrain their men, but since this was difficult to do, he therefore "preferred the inconvenience and privations of his present life to this obvious risk."[36]

The naval scientists were interested in Maquinna's house "which like all of those which compose the town, is twenty-two metres long and fifteen metres wide, but its elevation does not correspond to these dimensions." The roof and walls were described as being made of well-joined boards, supported on beams for the entire length of the building, and sustained by heavy columns of unfinished pine in its natural form. In the four corners of the house were four separate living quarters, occupied, as the Spaniards thought, by related families or by servants of the chief. On one wall could be seen two large figures, "which imitated with considerable fidelity the human body." This was a customary decoration of Nootkan homes, but the significance of these figures was not learned by Espinosa and Cevallos, since they "did not dare to inquire" of their host.

Following the visit to Maquinna's home, the Spanish lieutenants paid their respects in the home of Canapi [Anape], father of Maquinna's first wife, who was a subordinate chief in Nootka. Canapi was not home, but his eldest son, Keiskonuk, bedecked in a "costly cape of the finest sea otter," came forward to receive the visitors, a courtesy which on this visit Maquinna had not demonstrated.

During the entire visit to Tahsis village, the Iberian mariners found themselves continually surrounded by Maquinna's subjects, who harassed them from all sides, and who impeded their examination of things of interest. The mariners did get the opportunity to walk the length of the village, a distance estimated at 630 metres. The houses were characterized as of symmetrical architecture, offering a quite agreeable aspect despite their simplicity. Almost all were noted to have elliptical or square windows, and in one of the windows there was glass, just like that used by the Spaniards. It seemed strange to the visiting mariners that the Nootkans were possessors of so much by way of European trade goods that they were in a position to sell them.[37] The local natives had come to a point where, after several years of trade with the White man, they had grown tired of glass objects and of trade beads, customary goods of commerce. Even iron instruments had failed to remain economically desirable to them, nor had they been sufficiently attractive to be introduced into local artisanry. These facts gave rise to the following evaluation:

We know that abundance decreases the value of all those things which have a purely conventional appeal; nevertheless, and even though it is not easy to estimate the influence of fashion, it can be assured that copper and Monterey shells [abalone] will remain for some years the articles most treasured at Nootka Entrance. Upon this principle any system of commerce which is considered for establishment on this coast ought to be based.

Realizing by then that it was late afternoon and since the mariners wanted to reach Esperanza Inlet before nightfall, they returned to their launches. Maquinna, who had never left their sides while they were on land, came out to the boats with them. There the chief and the visitors parted, but not until Maquinna had been the recipient of additional presents. The farewell scene also gave rise to a brief physical description of the Overlord of Nootka, one in which he did not fare as well as in some others, hardly according in detail with the more complimentary accounts of other journalists.

The age of this chief, whose name is repeated with great frequency and even greater respect at Nootka Entrance, is not over thirty years. He is of short stature and is ill-formed in the lower half of his body, but he makes up for these deficiencies with a spiritual air, full of majesty and nobility, with which he inspires naturally a respect for his person.

A frequent subject of inquiry was first broached by the two visiting officers, but they were unable to find out with any certainty anything relative to the custom attributed usually exclusively to Maquinna of eating human flesh. In this matter they deferred to Captain Cook, who had left no doubt that "this custom which degrades and dishonours the human species was common in the year [17]78 among all the inhabitants of Nootka." Concerning this inquiry the Spanish visitors remarked:

We had the same fate as in other things that we tried to ascertain: Our interpreter, who knew the Nootka language about as well as he knew Greek, generally didn't make himself understood, and to communicate we had recourse to actions, which having as arbitrary a meaning as the words, were not any better understood. Under these circumstances, we confess without embarrassment that having been in Tahsis little more than an hour, we are not able to say anything with certainty concerning the religious ideas of these people, of their civil government, nor of the jurisdiction of Macuina over the neighbouring chiefs. Nevertheless, our landing at this village may have some real utility: Gentle and generous conduct has perhaps destroyed some sinister opinion that these men might have of the Spanish, which could never be advantageous to our country which attempts with such diligence and at such costs to maintain settlements in those places.

Another item noted by these early visitors was Maquinna's treasure, consisting in considerable measure of sheets of copper; but at the same time they noted and could not help lamenting the fact that they did not see in Maquinna's home any other provision for sustenance for the entire family than a great quantity of mussels that were being roasted.

In calculating the total population of Maquinna's domain, Cevallos and Espinosa guessed that it would be approximately four thousand for all of the villages combined, which were "so situated in the most part to live upon a not very abundant fishery, and alternating their residence according to this necessity, toward the seashore in the summer and toward the interior canals in the winter."

After having given presents prodigiously to all the chiefs and to the four wives of Maquinna, the visitors embarked in the launches. After exploring another canal, now called Zeballos Inlet, which was to the west, but led to the north, they went on to the Puerto de Esperanza, making a map with all the exactness that the short time available to them permitted. They finally returned to Friendly Cove by the outside passage, marking out while doing so the shoal that was explored by Captain Cook, which he had located at a much greater distance from the land than it really is.

Interior of Maquinna's house at Tahsis. This sketch shows the chief himself, dressed in a large sea otter robe, performing a dance during the visit of Quadra and Vancouver in the autumn of 1792. Drawing "finished" by José María Vasquez from a sketch by Atanasío Echeverría. (Archivo General y Biblioteca, Ministerio de Asuntos Exteriores.)

Apparently, this brief and pleasant visit on his own terrain was sufficient to reduce Maquinna's fears somewhat, but not quite enough to induce him to pay a visit to the large vessels for several days. Following subsequent contacts by other lesser native leaders, he made his first appearance at Yuquot on 18 August, which event was recorded by Lieutenant Secundino Salamanca:

The natives each time more satisfied by our kindly intentions kept repeating their visits, and all of their chiefs have permitted themselves to be seen. The one who all consider as their principal chief was here today, later bringing three of his four wives, who for some time were alongside; but it was not possible to make them come aboard, no matter how hard we tried to make them understand that it was only for the purpose of drawing them, and that we had given prodigally to those who had showed such courtesy.[38]

The following day aboard the *Descubierta* the same subject of portraiture was noted in the guard book by Midshipman Fabio Ali Ponzoni:

Maquinna, principal chief of the tribe of Indians that has dealings with our people, was aboard with one of his brothers and some other people. They were given various trinkets, by which attraction he yielded to our insistence that he bring some of his wives so they could be drawn. In fact, he came with three of his wives, whom he had left beforehand on a nearby point, after having become aware of our peaceful intentions and even more so of our friendliness toward him and his people. It was not sufficient, however, to permit them to come aboard, and without allowing us time to draw them, he went off to his rancheria.[39]

The principal chief of Nootka also visited aboard the *Atrevida* on the same day, accompanied by "one of his brothers," a young man of 15 to 16 years of age, and by two servants. Aboard both corvettes he received abundant presents, "without there being noted in him the least demonstration of generosity or even of appreciation."[40]

At 2 P.M. Maquinna bade goodbye to the Spaniards aboard the *Atrevida*, from which it appeared that he would return to Tahsis. Instead, however, he was soon seen returning with three of his wives "whom we infer he had left behind the nearby point doubtless with the object of gathering the fruits of his expedition in two places. In fact, he would have immediately achieved his premeditated design, if his too distrustful and too careful character had permitted them all to come up aboard, which with offers of further presents we suggested that they do; but it was not possible to get things to that point, depriving us consequently of drawing a picture of one of them who was young and very good looking."

While he was alongside, Maquinna tried to put on all the air of importance appropriate to his status, and one of his wives, "doubtless the most favoured, though not of the greatest merit," ate with him some little fruit from a basket. She picked out with great care the ripest ones, and gave them in the palm of her hand to Maquinna, "with both carrying out perfectly their respective roles."[41]

By this time Malaspina was confident that good treatment had done much to better relations with the natives. As early as Maquinna's first of several visits, Malaspina, in what was probably merited self-congratulation, said:

Our peaceful relations with the natives have at the present time established much more solid roots, although at the cost of some presents which the chiefs and subjects asked for indiscriminately, in addition to a continual contribution of biscuit.[42]

Tova added his comments:

Our efforts to gain the confidence and friendship of the natives had not been unfruitful. Their canoes, which previously fled from the sight of our small boats, now surround them without the least misgiving. There was scarcely any chief who had not visited us several times, including the principal chief Macuyná, although without being able to disguise in his face the fear that gripped him.[43]

It was believed that self-interest rather than curiosity had motivated Maquinna's earliest visit, one during which he arranged for the sale of a young child of about 10 years of age, "stolen from the Nuchimares [*sic*]," to the Spaniards aboard the station vessel, the Frigate *Concepción*. Shortly after arrival in Nootka the expedition had contact with the chaplain of the *Concepción*, Father Nicolás Loera, who "gave us six boys whom he had obtained through industry and interest, in exchange for guns." He had obtained them for the purpose of teaching them the catechism and instructing them in "the doctrines of our sacred religion" and then baptizing them. "His Christian charity gave us much satisfaction and stimulated us to follow his commendable project. There was among them one whom the sailors called 'Primo.' He displayed quite a little vivacity and already could pronounce some words in our language." He also told the visitors a hard-to-believe story that he had been destined to be a victim to be eaten by Chief Maquinna together with many others, and that this custom was practised with the younger prisoners of war, as well as about the ceremonies which were used in such a detestable and horrible sacrifice. Having discovered a way to escape, he took refuge on the Spanish vessel. This same day, when it was already night, two other children arrived, a boy and a girl, brother and sister, who had also escaped, so they said, from the fury of these barbarians. They said that they came from "the country of the Nuchimas [Kwakiutl], who inhabit the banks of a great lake seven suns distant from us."[44]

The Libro de Guardias of the *Descubierta* also notes in this regard that "we learned that during the morning there had been an Indian woman at the [military] establishment. She was the mother of two children who some days earlier had been stolen by the Nootka Indians who had sold them to our people aboard the *Concepción*. She let it be known that she had come from very far off, and her hunger and fatigue told of how much she had risked out of her maternal love. They clothed her, and she became content and willing to follow the lot of her children." This example was both pleasing and surprising to the visitors.[45]

The actions of the Spaniards in purchasing young Nootka children, or children enslaved by the Nootkans, were by the time of the Malaspina visit a well-established practice. Whether from pious religious ideas or because it had become a matter of policy, the number of natives of this type who had been carried off, including members of both sexes, had reached twenty-two. Most were destined for San Blas, the Spanish naval base in Nayarit, and their education and future care entrusted to some one or another of the naval officers of known good conduct who lived at that town, but always under the condition of these exiles receiving absolute liberty when they reached adulthood.[46] Malaspina, a man of liberal ideas for his time, seemed opposed to this traffic and indicated that "this type of trade is too tied up with ideas of religion, morality and government to be able to discuss it in a few lines."[47]

Malaspina learned, as had others, that the price for each had been one or two sheets of copper, and at times some shotgun or musket, or a few metres of cloth. The humanitarian feelings of the visitors were evident in Malaspina's statement, in which his liberal ideas are also evident:

It would not be boldness to assert that the children, even in their social situation, were greatly bettering their fate, even though the recriminations against Mocuina concerning his propensity toward being a cannibal were untrue; but the natural repugnance toward slavery of one's fellow humans and the fear that the trustees of these children might under the cloak of religion try to justify a type of permanent dominion over these unfortunate beings, induces us to desire either that a limit be placed on these acquisitions or that the law concern itself with their future well-being with attention to the inclinations that motivate them, to the purity of our religion, and to the inalienable rights of man.

Malaspina felt that the source of supply of many of these children was from the "Iquates nation." In fact, for this and other reasons, Malaspina felt that if it were not for the presence of the Europeans in Yuquot, and of their alliances with Maquinna, which gave that chief preponderance of force over his enemies, trouble would break out. Maquinna's economy would be much more secure if it were not so dependent upon fishing and were to be turned to raising of crops and tending of livestock. To the visiting naval scientist it seemed that "despite the barbarous custom of stealing children, or of neglecting or abandoning them, the people of Nootka can doubtless be considered as quite advanced in civilization, if they are to be compared to the others who people the eastern shores of the Pacific Ocean north of the Tropic of Cancer. At least these suggestions do not seem unsuitable when we consider that Mocuina no longer values anything

except glass for windows, firearms and blue cloth, and that Tlupanunulh desires nothing besides gunpowder, canvas sails and hemp lines for the use of his canoes."

There was frequent opportunity, as indicated in the Guard Books of the twin corvettes, for the Malaspina expedition to ameliorate the strained relationship between the garrison and the natives. As early as 17 August, according to Suria,

we noticed that the natives were losing their fear which the outrage that had been committed by Martínez, in the killing of Chief Callicum, had produced in them. Whenever those natives thought about him, they displayed the most extreme desire for vengeance. They now approached us with familiarity and assured us that their principal *tais* or chief would come to visit us. [Meanwhile] the noble Tlupanamibo [Tlupananulg] was lodged on the beach at the establishment where at certain hours of the day he sang for us in company with his oarsmen about the glories of his nation and of his ancestors, and at other times about his own feats and military exploits, all in a meter like the anacreontic. When he got to these last songs, this old man took on such vigour and enthusiasm that he was able to represent perfectly with his actions the struggles, the leaping, the dismay of his enemies and all that could give a true idea of his particular triumphs.[48] At 4:30 P.M., he prepared his canoe for his return, leaving as a hostage a son of his and the square box until his return with the Emperor Macuina. He went away with great swiftness. I drew a portrait of him which was much praised for its likeness to him in his features.[49]

Of special interest was another visit by the same chief, Tlupananulg, who had earlier been asked to pay a visit with his great war canoe. On 23 August the awaited visit materialized when the chief arrived at 7 A.M. with this native craft, bringing with him his aged father of some

65 years, three of his children and twenty strong Indians who acted as oarsmen. The huge war canoe approached with the rowers carrying out their efforts in time to a song "which was in no way disagreeable."[50]

Tlupananulg and his entourage made several turns about the Spanish vessels, rendered a salute with their oars in passing by, and carried out other interesting manoeuvres in time to the song, without losing a stroke of their oars. After an excellent approach to the *Atrevida*, the chief was presented with biscuit for his men and with a newly made sail which he intended to use on his war canoe.

Tlupananulg bade goodbye to the Spaniards aboard the *Atrevida* and went off to repeat the same manoeuvres and salutations for the benefit of the officers and crew of the sister ship. The mariners aboard the *Descubierta* also gave him liberal presents. All the natives reciprocated by holding a dance on the quarterdeck to the sound of some little sticks which were played in good time. After the native singing and dancing were concluded, the natives were given wine, biscuit and a knife for each person, and with this they were quite satisfied. The Spaniards were no less satisfied with this opportunity to obtain a "sufficiently exact idea of their diversions, and to have had the painter Suria make some pictures of this."[51]

As a last act, Tlupananulg directed his war canoe to shore where he paid a visit to Alberni, the popular commanding officer of the Catalonian Volunteers. After conclusion of this short stay, Tlupananulg, making use of his newly acquired sail, and "showing some evidence of capability in its management," set out for his village near the end of Tlupana Arm.

The Nootkans

On the same day, 23 August, Naneguiyus, son of Chief Canapi and brother-in-law of Maquinna, repeated an earlier visit that he had made, providing at this time a considerable amount of information for the Spanish visitors. "His vivacity and facility in explaining himself and our understanding him as well as his knowledge of the things of his country" permitted acquisition of additional knowledge of "rather curious things." The able young chief drew with his hand on paper a map of the channels, lakes and villages located on the bodies of water toward the interior of the area, including the area of the "Nuchimases with whom they carry out trade in copper and sea shells [from Monterey] for sea otter pelts."

From this description, in which Naneguiyus was aided by Natzape, the Spaniards received very specific information from which it was determined that those trading partners were located northnortheast from Friendly Cove. When Maquinna and his Nootkans went there to trade for sea otter pelts, they left Tahsis and travelled by land for two days over bad trails, carrying on their shoulders their small canoes, a supply of copper, shells and other trade goods. They arrived at a round lake and went directly across it. The first lake communicated by means of a rapidly flowing channel with a colder second lake, both of fresh water. They had difficulty in the very narrow channel, with a possibility of losing their canoes to the swift current, against which they could only with difficulty gain headway, and even then they needed to use a line ashore and be partly pulled. It was in these rapids that Natzape had lost his favourite wife while on a recent trading trip. In this manner Maquinna's trading party would take two days to make this passage. They would come out afterwards to another lake, much greater than the first, which they would also traverse, staying close to the shore. This took four days, with the nights being spent ashore. Finally, entering another narrow canal which was without current, they headed for the villages where the principal chiefs of the Nuchimas Indians resided, there to gain the advantage of trade, which took the form of mutual gift giving. En route some other Nuchimas villages along the shore of the previously traversed lake were bypassed.

Since the Nootkans only measured their distances by the number of days or suns that were spent in travel, it was impossible for the Spaniards to determine the distance involved in these trading expeditions. But by computing that on the average they could not travel between the water and land routes described more than eight to ten leagues per day, the Malaspina group was of the opinion that the distance could not have been less than 80 to 100 leagues in total.[52]

On 25 August, a few Nootka canoes were alongside the exploratory vessels. To these the Spaniards made known their desire to receive a final visit from Maquinna before the impending resumption of their round-the-world exploring expedition. Among other stated motives was the desire to make him happy and to give him presents "because to us his friendship was much more important than that of the rest of the chiefs." To the end of sending the appropriate message to Chief Maquinna, the officers of the *Atrevida* attempted to call some of the fishing vessels that were passing by the mouth of Friendly Cove, so that one of them might serve as messenger; but it was not possible to make them come alongside. Rather, to the contrary, they went off rowing with greater speed.[53]

On 26 August, there were several visitors of importance, and it is presumed that Maquinna received his invitation through them. In the morning Keiskonuk was aboard the *Atrevida*, while in the afternoon Michinish, "the brother of Maquinna," was aboard the same corvette, while Naneguiyus went aboard the *Descubierta*. The Spaniards made inquiries about various aspects of Nootkan culture, including funerary rites of the nobility.

The death of Macuina and of his relatives is celebrated with a universal crying. All of the Indians carry him in two lines to the edge of Conuma [Peak]. The Nuchimases come by invitation. They call him several times. He does not answer. They enclose him fully in a high box. From there it takes [the chief's spirit] nine days of great fatigue and without eating to arrive at the sun, where he finds joined together all of the Michimis [commoners] and the members of his family. They receive him as a friend, they give him things to eat. They are again transformed to bodily substance. He sleeps again the same way with his wives when they die and go there; but they never again return to this world, and are there thus eternally. The good are not distinguished from the bad in the future life. Although someone might have killed Macuina, when he arrived there they would greet each other like friends, and all discord would end. They say that those who accompany the corpse sing with great grace in the same way that we sing *Salve Virgen pura*. It seems that the Chief is the high priest because he is the one who does everything.[54]

In dealing with the burial customs of the Nootkans, another document adds the following:

He (Maquinna's brother-in-law) says that those who accompany the corpse sing as they go. Some of the Michimis have their tongues cut out, and they make various incisions in their chests all the way into the interior part of the upper body cavity. They place on him [Maquinna] an undershirt or tunic. They place a canoe at the spot of burial, and they sit on their haunches.

The same document adds some general details about Nootka culture:

They divide time by moons. Their periods of time consist of ten moons, and they call it a sun. They do not count higher than ten. They enjoy wine, calling it Spanish water. Macuina has only one true brother. The Tais can have three wives: forsaking always the one which is pregnant, they have intercourse with the others. The Michimis are not permitted more than one.[55]

On 27 August, the last full day that the Spaniards were in Nootka, the much desired final visit of Maquinna occurred. This was preceded by a visit earlier in the day by Natzape, "Chief of the Nuchimases, whose confederacy we managed to win over by means of some presents." From these two final visits, and doubtless from the earlier one of the highly respected Naneguiyus, the Spaniards obtained some more detailed knowledge of Nootka ethnology. One of these sources is entitled "Apuntes incordinados acerca a las costumbres, usos, y leies de los salvajes havitantes del Estrecho de Fuca [Uncoordinated notes concerning the customs, usages, and laws of the savage inhabitants of the Fuca Strait]," which has as its first subheading "Noticias que nos dió Maquina [Information that Maquinna gave us]." Thus the principal chief, as had earlier been hoped, became a direct informant for scientific study by the Malaspina group.[56]

Events of the long and important day of 27 August began when the bearskin-clad Natzape climbed aboard the *Atrevida*. The Spaniards understood that his ceremonial dress was the sign of sovereignty among the people of the Northwest Coast and was a required costume for important events. The Spaniards felt that this visit by Natzape was independent of the later visit by Maquinna, but there seems no doubt but that it was preliminary. Ciriaco Cevallos was the officer of the day aboard the *Atrevida*, and since he had already visited Maquinna at Tahsis during his reconnaissance with Espinosa, he was perhaps more familiar with the Nootkans than most of the other officers. At any rate, "taking advantage of his [Natzape's] good will, we acquired the information that is written below in the same order in which we learned it or in which the questions were asked."

The inhabitants of Nootka have no clear ideas of God as creator of all things, but give a certain type of interior worship to the spirit of their taises [chiefs], who from their heavenly abodes preside over all objects of creation. The winds blow at their will: They rule the universe and they communicate to man through thunder. The custom of apotheoses introduced to the ancient people of Egypt and Greece through the memory of some beneficent Kings, seems to extend itself to the inhabitants of Nootka and to all the chiefs, whether good or bad, without exception. We do not know if these chiefs work in concert together in heaven, or whether they divide out the control of nature. Nor were we able to learn whether they receive some exterior worship and if they have some men set apart privately for employment as religious ministers and to interpret the words of the gods.

The knowledgeable Natzape added to the information previously obtained concerning the ceremony that would occur at the death of Maquinna or other important chiefs.

As soon as the chief dies and before ascending into heaven, he remains four days at Tahsis and another four at Conuma, the place where the bodies are deposited. The wives of the chiefs have after death a less happy destiny than their husbands. They remain in Tahsis itself, where they live invisible, but sometimes they allow their songs filled with softness and sweetness to be heard. It does not seem normal that the privilege of hearing them should be extended to everyone, for it is naturally the

The canoe is clearly that of Tlupananulg, but the background is the Spanish establishment at Núñez Gaona at Neah Bay, Washington. Ink drawing by José Cardero. (Museo de América 2.269; Palau 65, Sotos 633)

reward of those men who deserve the protection of the Gods, etc. All religions have their visionaries.

Concerning the fate of the souls of departed Nootkans, Lieutenant Viana added a few details. After the normal eight-day period after death, which was divided equally between the mountains of Tahsis and of Conuma, the spirit of the deceased chief flies like dust to a region in the atmosphere, where the sun is always to be seen, and where the food is always meat. If, indeed, the tais is killed violently, he is immediately placed at Conuma, where his head is severed from his body and the head returned to his home, where it is preserved in a hanging position and sung to continually for a period of ten days. At the end of that time, the head becomes invisible and flies off to the region destined for the taises.

In contrast to what the previous day's informants had suggested, Natzape said that the commoners of Nootka society did not have such a pleasant future to look forward to after death. When they died, as the Spaniards understood, they descended to the centre of the earth where they grazed like animals, ate lice and were condemned to live in a perpetual absence of sun.

Cevallos entered into the guard book for 27 August an unusually long section concerning Nootka mores, as well as expressing his personal philosophy, both of which seem largely out of place in a normal ship's record book.

No matter how little one reflects on the origin and progress of the first human societies, it is perceived that distributive and civil laws are seen to precede criminal laws; nevertheless we only acquired from Anazapi [Natzape] information concerning the latter. He who kills another pays for his crime by ten days of imprisonment, but the reincidence of this crime is paid for irrevocably by death. The thief has his hair cut off as well as the fingers of his hands, his face is scarified, and with these indelible marks of infamy, they exile him as unworthy to live in society.

Adultery is punished in men with death, this punishment being modified in women to that of four days' exile. If the adulterer is some chief and the adulteress is the wife of another chief, they join the offender and the offended, they castigate them with words, and the offenders are then separated forever. The rights of succession to the throne among the Nootkans follow the same order as among us. When a legitimate heir is lacking, the people gather together and elect the new sovereign by a plurality of votes. The measurement of time is governed by the movement and phases of the moon, in which matter the information of Natzape and Naneguiyus are in complete conformity. They do not possess sufficient knowledge to determine solar years, and solar altitudes are probably the only method they have to divide the day, measure time and arrange the events of civil life, etc.[57]

Turning to other fields of inquiry, Malaspina also recorded, with some variation, what had been said previously about burial customs, with only the question unanswered as to whether the customs would have been the same if chiefs other than Maquinna were the subject of funeral pomp. Variant details of Maquinna's future funeral procession indicated that "four lines of canoes, two to the right and two to the left, accompany the canoe which served as hearse. The singing is continuous and mournful; there are neither victims, nor offerings of food. When the party arrived at Conuma, they called him [Maquinna] again, and upon his failing to answer, they immediately proceed to shut him up completely in a box, without any other ceremony whatever, and finally to elevate the box on high, leaving it in approximately the same position as those at Port Mulgrave" among the Tlingit. In the afterlife Maquinna would not be joined by his wives, according to Malaspina, but since "they would be in a place not

*A woman of Nootka wearing a woven cedar bark cape and tunic,
possibly with strips of fur woven in. Ink and wash drawing attributed to
Tomás de Suria. (Museo Naval MS 1725 (4) Fig. la; Higueras 2941,
Sotos 607)*

very far away, there would be the satisfaction of hearing them sing
from time to time, and to obtain from this the sweet memory of past
marital faithfulness." Natzape, who, as previously noted, had lost his
favourite wife the previous year when on a trading trip into the
Nuchimases area his large canoe filled with treasure and carrying his
wife had overturned, with tear-filled eyes told the Spaniards that at
the very moment he could hear his wife singing.

From these ideas of the role of women in Maquinna's funeral and
in the life of Natzape, the visitors felt that contact with new ideas had
introduced those concepts into Nootka thinking. Perhaps also as a
result of the fact that Malaspina's informant was the chief who had
lost his wife, the role of women in the funeral rites was being
overemphasized.

From the same Natzape, it was learned that one of the reasons for
plural marriage among the chieftains was a prohibition from intercourse when the women were still nursing their babies, as well as a
disdain for intercourse with wives who were very far advanced in their
pregnancies. Each wife of the chief slept on her own mat in one of the
four corners of the apartment, and the husband visited at his election
one or the other. This was done in silence, taking advantage of the
darkness, employing modesty, and also using those "caresses which
emanate from married love and distinguish us in this way from the
beasts."

"A Banquet of Human Flesh"

Nootka inhabitants did not eat human flesh, if one is to believe
Natzape, but Cevallos conjectured, since "this chief knows that the

Spaniards disapprove of and perhaps have punished this odious custom, nothing would be more natural that to deny it. This is a point that needs new information. Meanwhile and following the testimony of a traveller [Cook] whose authority cannot be more respected, it is necessary to believe that the Nootkans are anthropographi."

Malaspina was unconvinced and the important question claimed a great deal of his attention and speculation. Although his officers suspected that Maquinna did have cannibalistic tendencies, Malaspina was inclined to be more charitable toward the Tais of Nootka. He made a detailed inquiry of both historical and contemporary impressions, one certainly motivated in great measure by the fact that in the Spanish settlement at Santa Cruz de Nutka "everyone was firmly convinced" that Maquinna was a cannibal. At any rate, he had been accused so often as to make this a pressing question affecting the safety and the attitudes of the garrison at Friendly Cove.

Malaspina took to the inquiry willingly, if only for the purpose of refuting the opinions published by British Captain John Meares, "who methodically and fully asserted positive reasons to deduce the fact" of the chief's anthropophagy. "Captain Cook, who viewed with truly philosophical eyes the customs of the nations which he visited, must have been misled therefore by the great number of human bones, heads and hands that on several occasions were offered to him as items of trade." Malaspina reasoned that since even as late as his visit, and even if the natives treated their enemies in a brutally cruel manner, in no way different than that noted on earlier occasions, and universal among uncivilized men everywhere, that such treatment did not incriminate them of the strange inhumanity "which guides those who feed on human flesh out of sheer fancy."

Malaspina pointed out that during the year that the bogus "Dr. Maccay" lived at Nootka, left there in 1786 by merchant captain James Strange, the Indians were suffering from a great scarcity of food, but that there was never heard any suggestion of his being offered a sacrifice to this shortage, nor did Maquinna or any of the other chiefs partake of human flesh during that period. "It is to be supposed thus since Captain Meares would not omit such an important point in his article 'Story of Mr. Marcay [Maccay]', as it would tend to prove the custom of cannibalism among Maquinna and his subjects."

A second visit of Meares to Nootka had permitted him to revive the question of cannibalism. Meares decided on the basis of testimony of Anapi and Callicum, as well as upon his own observations, that not only was Maquinna a cannibal but also that the other tribal chiefs joined him monthly by private invitation.

Common belief at the Spanish settlement was almost identical with that of Meares. Malaspina attributed the local opinion as more the result of dissemination of the idea by the time of a meeting at Nootka of the fur trading vessels *Ifigenia, Argonaut, Lady Washington* and *Columbia*.[58] Maquinna's alleged propensity for human flesh was attested to by the declarations of various young children sold to the Spaniards aboard the vessel *Concepción*.

One of these said that Macuina truly liked human flesh, and that the selection of the child for this horrible banquet depended on the direction of the chief's hand while he was blindfolded. But this does not bring to mind in any way either the ceremonies that Captain Meares describes or the use of adult men, nor finally the participation of the other chiefs. Our officers have already charged him and even threatened him, but he nevertheless continued to deny this deed with as much consistency as our people maintained in believing it to be true.

Possessed of this background information, Malaspina felt that his expedition's inquiries on this point would be easy, and therefore to have omitted such investigation would have been unforgivable, since the natural scientists considered that they were working for the common knowledge of mankind.

At the present time our first indications showed us that we had no other data up to now with which to incriminate Mocuina of this strange offense except the simple account of a child (of 8 or 9 years of age), whose interpretation was doubtful. Different visits to his village since the establishment of our fort have never provided the least indication either of the existence of this terrible repast of victims, or of the fragments of a recent sacrifice of this type. Finally, the more we become acquainted with the friendly character of the other chiefs of this nation, the more we are disposed to clear them of this inhuman act.

In a footnote, Malaspina added: "It could be appended that Mr. Ingraham, the pilot of the *Columbia*, describing in a letter to Pilot Martínez everything that he had observed among these natives over the long period of a winter, did not indicate the least suspicion of this horrible inclination of Maquina."

From all the above reasoning, if cannibalism existed, it was confined to the case of Maquinna alone. In pursuing the matter, Malaspina took heed of the information gathered from local informants.

Our inquiries with the natives had equal success. In asking the young Teyocot, brother-in-law of Macuina, what were the foods of the chief, he always completed his listing in naming fish, deer, herbs and roots, without ever even remotely mentioning human flesh. Nanikius [Naneguiyus], who at first answered affirmatively to our questions, very

quickly convinced us that he had misunderstood, and rejected with horror even the idea of such an invitation. Finally, Natzape, with whom for a long time we engaged in sad reminiscence of the arrival of Captain Cook at this port, assured us that the hands, heads and bones presented aboard the Resolution, were nothing more than the remains of his enemies, and that it would not be strange to see on the hands the evidence of a few bites, because the infuriated Michimis used to take out in this manner the extremely vehement impulses of their anger. Neither he, nor Mocuina, would be capable of making a banquet of human flesh, an idea which disgusted him extremely, making him frequently use the words *Pishek, Pishek*; bad, bad, and even to tell Mocuina (who a little later incidentally came aboard the *Descubierta*) of the unjust suspicions that we had formed concerning him.[59]

A footnote was added concerning Natzape's knowledge of Cook's visit to Nootka: "Natzape, although at the time a young man of only 13 or 14 years of age, preserved very well in his memory various events of that expedition. The house and rancheria visited by Captain Cook were those of Calacan [Callicum]. He recognized a portrait of the Captain; he named without aid Captain Clerke, and asserted his belief that Lieutenant King was the son of Captain Cook."

In further pondering the cannibalism question, Malaspina indicated that there was never to be noted among the Michimis the least sign of hatred toward their Chief Maquinna. To the contrary, during the visit of Espinosa and Cevallos to Tahsis, those officers could not cease to admire the pleasure with which his subjects responded to his desires. Nor did this early Spanish party in their unexpected visit in Maquinna's home, his armoury and his treasure house notice "the least evidence of human fragments."

An analysis of Captain Meares's reasons in support of his opinion was advanced to support the new hypothesis of non-cannibalism. The first motive ascribed by Malaspina to Meares was the English mariner's interpretation of Maquinna's confusion when the chief presented the hand and ring of the unfortunate Mr. Millar of the trading vessel *Imperial Eagle*. The Spanish commander reasoned that Maquinna could hardly have been the person who had eaten the flesh of that officer, since the murder had been perpetrated on the shores of another "kingdom," south of the Strait of Juan de Fuca. The declarations of Anapi and the deceased Callicum are "difficult to reconcile with the character which the selfsame Captain Meares attributes at least to the latter, and surely if we were to judge by appearances, it would seem more probable that the one who feasted on human flesh would be the one who rested his head on a basket of human fragments [Callicum], rather than the one who sucked the blood from his own wound, although he might have appeared to have enjoyed it." Finally, that Maquinna should have boasted to Meares about the recent celebration of one of the banquets, and "suddenly attributed this cannibalistic orientation to all of the tribes of Nootka, except the beneficent Callicum, does not harmonize with either the hunger that Mr. Maccay observed in the winter of [17]86, or with the source or depository of so many slaves that one should therefore suppose existed." With this conclusion, Malaspina laid to rest his considerable preoccupation with this topic.

The Realm of Maquinna

In commenting on the extent of Maquinna's domain, Malaspina saw it as extending to approximately the area explored by his two officers, Espinosa and Cevallos, during the reconnaissance of the interior canals. Its limits were thought to be Punta Rompientes (Breakers Point), the villages of Yzcuates (probably dependent on rival chief Wicannanish of Clayoquot), other tribes to the northwest or Cabo Frondoso (Woody Cape), which locations it was not easy for the Spaniards to learn, and finally to the back part of the Nuchimases' land, the number of whom and their power were seemingly very superior to those of Nootka.

The chiefs of other areas or districts were subordinate to Maquinna. They in turn had a certain number of subjects who obeyed them in the private matters of society. They only had to join together for causes of common defense or in attacks on their enemies. "These subordinate chiefs, either by accident, or by regulation, or by convenience derived possibly from previous bloody wars, are interrelated by means of marriages," but "the supreme power resides in the person of Macuina, who for his part presides over the rancheria at the head of Tahsis Canal, and over those which are scattered over the large island that makes up the Port of Yacuat [Nootka Island]."

Malaspina named the subordinate chiefs of Nootka as just three: Natzape, "Tlaparanalh," and "Calacan," the latter having been killed by Martínez. To this he added: "We are far from wishing to justify the conduct of Pilot Martínez on that occasion, but by the incidental information of Natzape at the present time, we see that Captain [John] Meares has charged this event with some unnecessary additions," though Malaspina did not specify those attendant circumstances. The scientists did not find out who had succeeded to the power held by the murdered chieftain, but they did learn that Tlupananulg was earlier also called Calacan. This custom of name changing makes positive identification of early Indian leaders very difficult, particularly after the passage of two centuries.

It was evident that Maquinna and his subordinate chiefs and their families formed the tais class, or nobles, destined to govern the plebeians, the Michimis. "Both laws and religion combine to make this difference more pronounced."

Among weak tribes who are fishermen, and so constituted as to go to war frequently, it ought not to appear strange that when the chief reaches an age of incapacity to direct public actions with bravery, valour and example, he turns over the government to his son. We were not able to ascertain this concerning Maquinna, because we think that his father is not alive; but certainly Anapi [Canapi], father of Natzape, and the father of Thipananulh [Tlupananulg], who came aboard amidst the Michimis, no longer enjoy either the respect or the authority that is given to their sons. Nor were we able to ascertain whether the women enjoy the right of succession. It is quite probable that it is not so, if we can judge from the little appreciation that this pleasant half of the species rates from them.

It was learned that in case Maquinna's line should be extinguished, there would be an election of a new ruling house, something that "has not come to pass up to the present." The outcome would depend on the vote of the commoners, and once completed and agreed upon, the new line would enjoy all the prerogatives of sovereignty and of the priesthood which were the attributes of this position. The Spaniards did not learn who, or what group, takes the reins of government if the heir apparent, upon the death of his father, was not old enough nor had the necessary qualities for command.

Other expedition journals noted that Maquinna's successor would come from among his sons, and lacking sons, the next in line would be the eldest brother of Maquinna, followed in turn by the sons of the eldest brother. In this succession to the throne, only the children of Maquinna by his first wife could become monarchs, though all of his children were taises. His children's children would also be of that same socio-political class.[60]

Be the succession question as it may, Viana added, "these people love their chief, and in the respect and subordination that all profess for Macuina, as well as in the propriety and government of this chief, there stands out doubtless an advance in society which in our thinking cannot be reconciled with either their substance or their lack of clothing."

A Pact Confirmed

Maquinna, in response to the repeated entreaties of the Malaspina group and of its desire to leave well cemented the friendship of that chief with the Spanish settlement at Santa Cruz de Nutka, put in an appearance aboard the *Atrevida* later in the morning of 27 August, after the departure of Natzape. As commanding officer, Captain Bustamante, for whom Maquinna later professed great friendship, attempted to give the Nootka principal chief such presents as he was able in order to make the chief "understand how pleasing his friendship was, and that it should continue with the people of our settlement." Maquinna had several cups of tea with his European friends, "a custom found to be well introduced among his relatives and subaltern chiefs." The Nootkans were much more accustomed by this time to Spanish foods, including wine, beans and biscuit, whereas the Mulgrave Tlingit had shown an undisguised abhorrence as indicated by Dr. González when he said that "they did not like fresh bread nor hardtack; sweets and wine were repugnant to them; oranges caused them nausea; and, above all sugar was absolutely unbearable, the sensation of this condiment being so disagreeable on their system that after spitting it out and washing out their mouths they tried to clean their tongues by scraping them with the first object that they had at hand."[61]

The Spanish propaganda, born of a great desire to ratify their friendship with Maquinna and to "testify with presents of great value as to how much we were interested in the solidification of a reciprocal peace" with the Nootkans, had left no doubt in the natives' minds concerning the honesty of Spanish intentions.[62] Lack of Spanish interest in the acquisition of furs and the nearness of the departure date of the corvettes, which by then had already been reprovisioned with water and wood, tended to dissipate Maquinna's earlier fears. These reasons, "and even more so the hope of a fine gift, had in fact worked with great force on the heart of Macuina, and there could be read now very clearly on his face the desired change."

For the occasion of his final visit, Maquinna adorned his head with strips of grass onto which were sown some stars of glass. He alleged that his reasons for not visiting more frequently had been his preoccupation with fishing and his lack of robustness. This lack of strength he attributed to the fact that since the Spaniards had dispossessed him of his former habitation site at Yuquot so that they could build there the Spanish settlement, he had degenerated into his present weakness, which he thereupon demonstrated. Previously, Maquinna claimed, he had such strength that with "a single thrust of the harpoon he killed a whale, the size of which he showed us," and he indicated that today it would be impossible for him to do it, a story which he had rehearsed well.

In an effort to make Maquinna's situation more bearable, the gentlemanly Malaspina presented the Nootka chief with two canoe sails, four window panes, a sheet of copper, some yards of blue cloth and a few pieces of assorted hardware.[63] The commander of the round-the-world exploring expedition insisted to Maquinna that the chief reestablish his headquarters near the Spanish settlement, "assuring him that he would prohibit with the greatest strictness that any of the sailors should go to the Nootka houses." Since Malaspina was leaving, it is hard to determine how he could have seen to it that such a promise was implemented; the only fear that Maquinna had of the sailors was that they might solicit the Nootka women, but the chief reiterated that the officers had never occasioned the least offense. During the corvettes' stay at Nootka, there had been no report of any sexual solicitation, though trade contacts were many.

Malaspina made an offer to turn the Spanish settlement over to the Nootkans when the Iberians should finally some day retire from the area, with the big house, that used by the commandant, which was under construction in 1791 as can be seen in contemporary drawings, to go to Chief Maquinna and the other buildings to be divided among the other chiefs. To this promise the Overlord of Nootka responded by assuring his friendship and indicating that the Spaniards would always be the owners of the area which they at that moment occupied.[64] There was thus re-ratified, Malaspina emphasized, "on that occasion the cession of land which had previously been made for the present national establishment, [and Maquinna] assured us that there would be between both of us a lasting peace."[65]

In reconfirming the earlier land cession, Malaspina was departing from what has been thought to be Spanish custom in dealing with aboriginal people, insofar as it has been generally held that Spaniards paid little heed to aboriginal rights of land ownership. The move by the commander of the exploratory expedition was directly in line with the orders of his superior commander, Antonio Valdés y Bazán, Spanish Minister of the Navy, and with new norms for establishing sovereignty through simplified symbolic acts as had been done at Mulgrave.[66]

The importance of Maquinna as an ace-in-the-hole for Spain in the controversy over Nootka is evident from Spanish preoccupation with the legality and correctness of their pretensions in the Pacific Northwest. Although Maquinna's testimony had already been elicited for Spain's position in the Nootka Sound negotiations with Great Britain, Malaspina's clarification with Maquinna of the terms of the garrison's tenure was designed to leave no doubt about Spanish rights of ownership.

During the final visit, Malaspina and his officers also gained from Maquinna more general information on Nootka culture, including:

That the true God or most powerful one is in heaven and is called *awashlaij-himi*; and another one is called *awak-himi*, and the god of fish is called *ans-himi*. That this god appears in dreams to Maquinna when he prays to ask that the rain cease and that there be fish, etc., and that at all times that he is sleepless in prayer anyone who sleeps with his wife dies. Maquinna's family, which is at his side, commiserates with him during the difficult time he spends. He is shouting inside a large chest where there is painted an ugly, misshapen figure of a man.[67] He said that only the taises go to see God, and contrarily those who have committed some offense have their bodies devoured by wild beasts. All the women and the plebeians go to the depths. Only at the time of the full moon did Maquinna sleep with his wives, that is, four days a month, and no matter how much they, who are many, were always inviting him, he avoided a crime which it was believed cost one his life.[68]

In his rough notes Malaspina mentioned Chief Maquinna frequently, and though these comments never found publication, nor were even converted into smooth copies, they do give insight into the local scene, while illustrating the type of information the naval scientists were concerned with in their investigations.

Arrival of Maquinna...his misgivings, timid and distrusting character. He sings some verses which the Captain [Alberni] composed for him. He doesn't wish to introduce his wives. He sells a child. They serve him food. His cruel and tyrannical character. He justifies his not coming frequently because it was the fishing season.[69]

The reference here to verses that Captain Alberni composed introduces a contribution which has been considered as of more value in recovery of Spanish prestige among the Nootkans than the brief visit of Malaspina. Pedro Alberni had displayed prior to Malaspina's arrival considerable perception of native psychology. Taking advantage of Maquinna's insecurity, the army officer had worked out a clever stratagem to restore the native leader's lost confidence. In the dark days after the tragic death of Chief Callicum, Maquinna had broken all familiar communication with the Spaniards. Utilizing what little that was known of the Nootka language, the astute Alberni had composed a verse, "proclaiming the greatness of Maquinna and the friendship that Spain professed for this chief and for his entire nation." It proclaimed that "Maquinna, Maquinna, Maquinna is a great prince and friend of ours; Spain, Spain, Spain is a friend of Maquinna and of Nutka." At that time Maquinna was so impressed with his song that he requested multiple encores so that he could learn it by heart. He did so to the point that many months later when the Spanish naturalist José Mariano Moziño was at Nootka, he learned it from the chief and recorded it in his *Noticias de Nutka*.[70]

In summation, Malaspina came perhaps the closest to evaluating some of the inner conflicts that were shaping the personality of Maquinna.

The character of Macuina today is not easy to figure out. His temperament seems a mixture of cruelty, suspicion and intrepidity. But the natural course of his feelings must have been disturbed greatly on one hand by the anxiety of the Europeans to cultivate his friendship, by a treasure built up in a few years, by the discords which have occurred among the Europeans themselves, and perhaps by the suggestion of one or the other among them of obtaining the monopoly of furs, and on the other hand by the weakness of his forces, the punishments suffered, the usefulness of commerce, and much too frequent arrival of European vessels in those areas.

Trading with Nootka

In a summary document entitled "Political Examination of the Northwest Coasts of America,"[71] the commander of the Spanish scientific expedition discoursed at length concerning Nootka. At times this became an historical inquiry into local customs, at others it was an extension of thoughts previously expressed by others. In this document, Maquinna was frequently mentioned and certain aspects of Nootka ethnology were singled out for more extended treatment. Since trade on the Pacific Northwest Coast was of concern to the Spaniards, though not of importance to Malaspina's visit, he wrote concerning the law of supply and demand in an unsophisticated trading environment such as Nootka.

The value of iron has diminished in such a way that now this article can be considered as a secondary necessity among those natives: A thing which we could never imagine happening was that in Maquinna's rancherias at present a sailor was refused a fur in exchange for fifty Monterey shells....The shells, a short time ago, had no value whatsoever in Monterey: The slightest payment to a mission neophyte for picking them up was sufficient to collect hundreds of them, and even more so since their stage of calcification was of no importance though they had been lying for a long time on the beach. Along the entire coast they were accepted with equal eagerness. But the same ease of acquiring them has made our mariners from San Blas sell them poorly, there being cases of giving fifty shells for a fur, when in the beginning at Nootka, and recently [in July] at Prince William Entrance, one or two shells would get a fine fur.[72]

Malaspina felt that it would be easy to put the brakes on this abuse, and that the fur trade of the Pacific Northwest Coast could be more advantageous to Spanish colonists of the west coast of Mexico than to any other national group. The monopoly that the Spaniards had on the Monterey abalone shells, which were the only kind desired by the Nootkans though somewhat similar shells could be procured in the Southwest Pacific, the potential rapidity of action and little distance that the Spaniards would have to travel to obtain shells, copper and used clothing for protection against the weather, all would work to the advantage of the Iberians and to the disadvantage of competitors. It was further suggested that by using the San Blas naval vessels, Monterey would be supplied, and then the Northwest Coast trade could be carried out as an outward extension of their voyage before returning home.

Although not sanguine of the commercial possibilities of the maritime fur trade, and cognizant of the fact that the Spanish government had already granted a monopoly to Vicente Vasadre y Vega, Malaspina gathered some additional data, which he wrote up in an "Extract of what has occurred in the sea otter business beginning from 1784 up to the present on His Majesty's account."[73] Some information was collected and included in an "Extract of a plan developed to begin fur commerce between Mexico and the Philippines." Malaspina indicated that "trade in sea otters boils down to acquiring by the exchange of things of little value the furs of those animals, which transported to Canton acquire in that market the high value of 25 *pesos fuertes* each, based on the average price of those that have been sold up to now. It is obvious that to receive for a few shells or a few pounds of cloth or copper, or finally for a useless suit, a pelt the sale of which for 25 pesos is almost certain" was too good to believe. As in all human endeavours, there were a considerable number of thorns and difficulties.[74] One of these was the limited number of pelts; a second was the great competition for them; and the final one was the length of time before a profit could be realized.

One necessary item for trade was window glass to serve as gifts for the Nootka chiefs, especially Maquinna, who already had some panes in his longhouse. If furs obtained on the Pacific Coast were to be shipped to the Oriental market in an uncured condition, Malaspina suggested that they be stowed in the staterooms or above deck and that they should be taken out frequently for air and sunshine. In order to avoid moths, it was suggested that the furs be wrapped in packages containing wild rosemary that "abounds along the entire coast and is very aromatic." Malaspina further suggested that for sending such furs from Mexico City to Acapulco there was in the capital a tannery called La Yguera, situated in the Barrio of San Pedro and belonging to Melchor de Garay, which firm had sold 1070 pelts and had a complete knowledge concerning the business and was capable of instructing about it in the future.[75]

As for private participation in fur trading, members of the scientific exploring expedition were reported to have collected about 300 furs, the result of petty trade. When the crew members heard that the price of furs on the Canton market, the normal Spanish outlet, was depressed, some of them sold their pelts to others who speculated that prices might be improving, or at least they hoped so.

Preparations for Departure

After much inquiry, certainly more than they had been able to conduct while at Yakutat among the Tlingit, including botanical reconnaissance, hydrographic investigation and supporting illustrations by the artistic contingent, the work at Nootka was considered finished. The objectives of resupply of wood and water had been carried out, and the scientific mission had been accomplished as much as possible given the shortness of their stay. The significantly greater accomplishments while at Nootka were gained largely by greater security of the vessels when in port, having need for only minimal safety measures, and from the intervention of a cadre of local residents who were anxious to be as helpful as possible, and who had an accumulated fund of knowledge about a place where they had been stationed for longer than they had wished.

In addition to considerable special assistance given by the expedition's carpenters, blacksmiths and others who helped make and repair things for the establishment, Malaspina dispensed small kindnesses with his customary gentlemanly courtesy to the garrison in appreciation for its support during his visit. Shortly prior to departure, the commanding officer had the supply officers of both vessels draw up a list of provisions and equipment in order to "give to the fortification as much help as compatible with our needs."[76] These lists included pieces of woolen cloth, flannel, tar, some utensils for the sick bay, for the pilotage and for the boatswain's locker, plus a large quantity of broth tablets and a large amount of flour from the officers' mess. Also left behind were the medicines that the surgeons found useful for this climate and for the prevailing illnesses, four casks of commonplace San Lucar wine, and a month's supply of foodstuffs to tide them over until the anticipated return of the *San Carlos*, the vessel that had gone off for relief supplies.

A second listing of items given by Malaspina to the Frigate *Concepción* and to the "garrison of the fort in the Port of Yucuat of Nutka," added other provisions such as biscuit, dried vegetables, bacon and vinegar. Plates, cups, clay pots, iron hoops, barrels, cloth and clothing, hammers, paper, nails, metal plates, flags, lead lines and gun parts were listed among the items left behind. Specifically, it was noted that Alberni had been favoured with gifts of cigarette papers, files, flints, caps and cloth.[77] In addition, Malaspina entrusted to Alberni a Reaumur scale thermometer for the scientific purpose of maintaining a more accurate meteorological diary during the coming winter.[78] It is probable that Malaspina's group was reimbursed for some and perhaps all such items as were transferred, though the exact manner of accounting has not yet come to light.

In a summary statement of reciprocal aid, it was indicated that

our attentions for the well-being of the establishment had to be both varied and important. We gave them a substantial part of our foodstuffs, clothing, tobacco, medicine, tackle; we repaired their arms and farming tools and they were shown very usefully the way how with "pine needles" to make beer that we, as well as the French, call *sapineta*.

While at Nootka the Malaspina party had carried out some direct utilization of conifer leaves to manufacture a type of strong beer that was thought to have anti-scorbutic properties.[79] By the end of the eighteenth century it was reasonably conjectured that scurvy was caused by inadequate diet, but it was not yet widely established just what specific remedy was preferable. The British were convinced that citrus juice, fresh or preserved, was best. Most mariners were persuaded that fresh vegetables and fruit were useful, but other possibilities such as the Nootka remedy were worth investigating, though no final report was made on the merits of the concoction. On other occasions, the doctors dispensed lemonade to the corvettes' crews. Whether this was done in imitation of English efforts or as the result of general acceptance of lemon juice as an anti-scorbutic is not clear.

In truth, said Malaspina, whatever had been done for the Nootka garrison "was but a small repayment for the generosity that the troop and the seamen of the [Nootka] detachment displayed toward our people, giving them as many vegetables as their gardens could produce; and offering them as much help as they daily needed,... either for the different tasks of the service or in a methodical cutting of wood, in which they shared for the better conservation of the efforts of the soldiers and sailors of both corvettes."[80]

Malaspina might well have added the kindness of a daily supply of freshly-baked bread from the settlement's ovens.

A final presentation of many gifts to Maquinna on the last full day in port had the reported effect of carrying out one of the initial reasons for stopping at Nootka, that of "securing a lasting alliance with this prince who was the most powerful in those parts and whose friendship can be most useful to our settlement."[81] At last Maquinna bade the Spaniards goodbye, "manifesting toward us, with expressions difficult to mistake, as much gratitude and friendship in the end as he had shown evidence of annoyance and suspicion in the beginning."[82] In the months and years to come, when there was never the remotest possibility of their return, Maquinna looked back to the good days of the visit of his friends Malaspina and Bustamante, commanders of the *Descubierta* and *Atrevida*. It was a brief friendship, but one which had been almost wholly on Maquinna's terms and represented a time when Maquinna's star was in the ascendancy.

Malaspina's expedition headed southward towards the California capital of Monterey, where it stayed for two weeks and then continued to Acapulco to prepare for the trans-Pacific crossing which was next on the exploratory agenda. At some unspecified time, the commander realized that much exploration had been left unaccomplished, particularly a thorough search in the Strait of Juan de Fuca. Good fortune soon provided a remedy for this uncompleted task.[83]

Alcalá Galiano and the 1792 Reconnaissance

While Malaspina was carrying out his northern explorations, Viceroy Conde de Revilla Gigedo was laying plans for further exploration in northern waters. He had ordered construction of a schooner, the *Mexicana*, for exploratory purposes and had planned to place it under Francisco Antonio Mourelle, an experienced San Blas officer who had been several times along the Pacific Northwest Coast and was knowledgeable of the explorations, maps and accounts that had been turned in over the years to the Viceregal Archives in Mexico City. He had been a special assistant to the Viceroy, entrusted with compiling such information for future action. His activity resulted in a "Compendio de Noticias," an extract of all naval activity on the Pacific Northwest Coast up to 1790. This compendium was made available to those who had a need to know, including Malaspina. Mourelle was also the most experienced officer available to carry out the follow-up exploration contemplated by the viceroy.

Malaspina professed great confidence in both Mourelle and in the pilot, Juan Carrasco, who were to carry out the final search for the fabled Strait of Ferrer Maldonado. However, the naval scientist pointed out logically that any expedition to the inland waters behind Vancouver Island ought to be entrusted to officers who were experienced in more modern techniques of astronomy and map making.[1] He felt that two of his young officers, just promoted to commander with the same date of rank, would do a better job. Conveniently, Mourelle also became ill and his illness provided the proper entering wedge for a change. Malaspina also indicated that two vessels would be much more suitable than one for exploration of uncharted and potentially dangerous waters; two vessels would assure safety and provide mutual support. He convinced the viceroy that a second, almost

Num.º 2

CARTA ESFÉRICA

de los *Reconocimientos hechos en la Costa N. O.*

DE AMÉRICA

en 1791. y 92. por las Goletas Sutil y Mexicana
y otros Buques de S. M.

Salida de las Goletas

Islas de Berrejord

Islas de Lanz

C.º Scot

P.ª Mexicana

ISLA DE QUADRA Y

Bahia de los...

Cabo Frondoso

Canal de Olavide

R.º de Viana

C.º de Remolino

B.ºo de Salamanca

B.ºo de Quintana

B.ºo de Ali-Ponzoni

Brazo de Toba

Canal del Rio

B.ºo de Bustamante

B.ºo de Malaspina

P.ºo de Magallanes

Punta Sarmiento

I.ª de Concha

Pico de Tasis

Isla de Nutka

1.ª Catala

Brazo de Guaquinanix

Bocas de Masdarrelo

Bocas del Carmelo

P.ºo de Macuina

Entrada de Nutka

ARCHIP. DE CLAUCUAT

P.ºo de S.ª Estevan

Y NITINAT

VANCOUV

CANAL DEL ROSARIO

Bocas del Engaño

Canal

P.ª de Terron

ENTRADA DE JUAN DE FUCA

Isla de S.ª Juan

I.ª de Bonilla

P.ªa de Martinez

P.ºa de Moreno

Bocas de

I.ª de Tutusi

R.º Canel

I.ª los Descados

P.ºa de Alava

Ens.ºª de Davila

P.ª de los Ang.

Bahia de Quimper

Ens.ºª de Mogos. Vipi.

Ens.ª y R.º de los Martires

I.ª de Dolores

Canal de Hood

P.ºa de la Bastida

Canal del Alm.

P.ºa de Gray

OCÉANO SEPTEN...

Ens.ª de Malabrigo

identical vessel, the *Sutil*, should be rapidly constructed at San Blas. Command was changed from Mourelle to Dionisio Alcalá Galiano and Cayetano Valdés, two of the best officers of the scientific exploring expedition.[2] As seconds in command, two additional officers from the *Descubierta* and *Atrevida*, Secundino Salamanca and Juan Vernacci, were assigned to the new task unit. The small schooners carried minimal crews of about twenty, with at least one-quarter of them having been detached from the corvettes to join the *Sutil* and *Mexicana*. A final personnel change, one of extreme importance to the general record, and particularly to the pictorial record of the newly planned expedition, was the substitution of José Cardero for Pilot Carrasco. Carrasco possessed only the normal skills of an ordinary pilot, whereas Cardero was thought not only to be able to carry out those functions, but also to have the experience and expertise to turn his hand to other expedition functions. He became scribe, mapmaker and pilot, and, of maximum importance, he was the artist who left behind a rich legacy of drawings and paintings of the Pacific Northwest Coast. For Cardero, his appointment was a reward for past services with the major vessels, and a springboard to later promotion to officer rank in the Spanish navy.

At a later time it was alleged by Spanish naval authorities that the 1792 expedition was not connected to the Malaspina effort, but this was neither true nor was it ever intended that the second trip be anything other than a sub-expedition. Certainly Malaspina incorporated the information, charts, drawings and other scientific results obtained into the corpus of the larger expedition materials, not even bothering to identify materials as to source, since all were intended for the major work that was forthcoming: the report of the expedition. However, when Malaspina fell into disfavour, there was an absolute prohibition of mentioning his name even in any of the peripheral publications emanating from the expedition. When reference was absolutely necessary, he was referred to as "the commander" or "the captain."

The results of the 1792 summer voyage of the *Sutil* and *Mexicana* became of considerable interest for diplomatic negotiations involving Spanish rights in the Pacific Ocean and, more particularly, in the Pacific Northwest. Consequently, whether willingly or by force of circumstances, the idea of independence of the 1792 voyage was advanced. Alcalá Galiano, who later became responsible for publication of the results of the summer reconnaissance, wrote a letter in 1795 in which he stated that the voyage of the *Sutil* and *Mexicana* had been an official exploration undertaken under the direction of the Viceroy of New Spain, the Count of Revilla Gigedo, and that the party was no longer a portion of the Spanish Naval Scientific Exploring Expedition headed by Malaspina and Bustamante.[3] There is no evidence in the account kept in 1792 that such a divorce between this effort and that of Malaspina had taken place. To the contrary, the archives contain Malaspina's set of instructions to the new commanding officers dated 14 December 1791.[4] Thin as the pretense was, it accomplished its purpose in that the results of the sub-expedition were published in 1802. Malaspina's name was never mentioned. By that time he was a political casualty, consigned to incarceration in a damp, wind-swept prison on the northwest coast of Spain.

With completion of the companion schooner, the *Sutil*, and the change of command, the twin vessels set out from San Blas to Acapulco. They reached that more southeasterly port eight days after departure of the *Descubierta* and *Atrevida*. During the trip down the coast the mariners discovered that the two vessels did not sail well.

This chart of the descoveries made on the Northwest Coast of America shows the work of Alcalá Galiano and Valdés in circumnavigating Vancouver Island in the summer of 1792. Published in Relación del viaje hecho par las goletas Sutil y Mexicana en al año 1792, *volume 2. (Special Collections, Library, University of British Columbia)*

Several modifications, including raising the main deck 33 centimetres in order to provide greater storage space, were carried out at Acapulco. Lack of manpower placed the responsibility for alterations on the crews, and sailing was delayed until 8 March 1792, though the original intent had been to go north several months earlier. Malaspina, who by this time had left for Guam, had left behind in Acapulco useful equipment for the schooners. In addition to the normal supplies and equipment, each of the tiny vessels carried scientific instruments for mapping and other purposes and a supply of presents or trade goods. Each vessel had 68 sheets of copper, 18 hatchets, 80 strings of assorted beads, two boxes of hardware items and 150 kilograms of nails. The *Mexicana* cargo also listed 112 kilograms of iron.[5]

It took the 46-ton schooners more than two months to make the northbound trip, but on 13 May they entered port at Nootka where they found three Spanish vessels. The Frigate *Santa Gertrudis* (Captain Alonso Torres, a newcomer) and the Brig *Activa* were anchored. Also there was the Frigate *Concepción*, Eliza's vessel, which was the station ship.

Upon arrival at Nootka, the schooners were met by Chief Maquinna who came out in a canoe, accompanied by his relatives and friends, to intercept the inbound vessels. For his efforts at welcoming the group, Maquinna was presented with an axe, four knives and some pieces of assorted hardware. He recognized various members of the arriving party – Valdés, Vernacci and Salamanca (and probably Cardero, though it is not so stated) – whose absence of only a little over eight months was hardly enough to erase good memories. Alcalá Galiano was a newcomer, but it was not long before he was well accepted in Nootka society. After the initial contact, Maquinna

followed the schooners with great satisfaction to their anchorage. Again it was apparent that the little vessels were unsuitable for the task that lay ahead, nor would they be for another three weeks, time spent in repair and minor alterations.

As a result of his two visits to Nootka in the summers of 1791 and 1792, Lieutenant Salamanca composed a document concerning the customs, uses and laws of the native inhabitants of the Strait of Fuca. It reiterated contents of other documents but also said concerning Nootka hospitality that "knowing that there was a scarcity of food in our establishment,...Maquinna daily sent fish, prohibiting his people from accepting any presents."[6]

Of Nootka justice, Salamanca said that during their stay at Nootka, one of Maquinna's commoners had seized a little girl in the forest and raped her. Maquinna condemned him to death. While the sentence was being executed, the chief came to the Spanish establishment so as not to hear the screams of the unfortunate person and asked for bread and trifles to give that night to the family and thus console it. The following day the visitors saw passing by all the family of the deceased, on their way to a different village, "without ceasing to be subject to Maquinna who visited them unarmed and with confidence."

The Spaniards told Maquinna about another Nootka criminal who came to seek shelter with the visitors, and learning that the crime was only that of having made a dishonest fur deal, the Spaniards asked that his life be spared. Maquinna conceded this request, telling them that they should strip him, dress him like a Spaniard and keep him because he was no longer able to live with the Nootkans. Maquinna was reported to have asked the Spaniards for similar clemency for his people if an equivalent situation arose.

This style of "Nootka hat," with its whale hunt motif, is worn by a number of chiefs drawn by artists José Cardero and Tomás de Suria. (Museo de América 13.567)

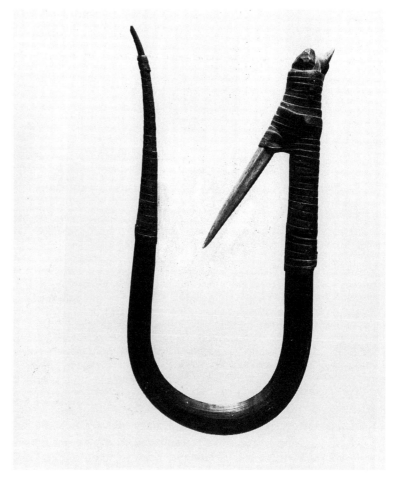

In addition to hats, helmets and armour, the expedition collected more utilitarian articles such as this halibut fishing hook acquired at Nootka. (Museo de América 2.883)

"Treated by us with extreme courtesy, they [the Nootka chiefs] always came with an air of pleasure and security. On hearing the dinner bell, Maquinna, wearing his hat, comes daily for a courtesy call and seats himself next to the commandant. He asks for what he wants. He uses a spoon, fork and glass very well. He asks for common wine or for full-bodied wine, and coffee at the end, if there is any; and chocolate for breakfast. Some days he gives fish. He did so on the Day of San Fernando when he knew that there was a guest on board and he put on his regal pelt."

Salamanca also commented on ceremonies which the natives put on for the benefit of the visitors, one in which Chief Chicomasia, who did not figure greatly in the 1791 visit, was a major participant.

Chicomasia gave a dance for us in his village [of Malvinas] in which I saw for the first time all the customs of the chiefs at these functions. They seated us there on benches covered with new matting, they passed out little sticks, they began their sounds and singing, they scattered many bird feathers and Chicomasia himself put on various masks of animal figures that they know, trying to imitate their voice and walk. Having finished, one came out into the middle and faced the commandant and shouted 'Quadra, Chicomasia gives you this': He showed eight good sea otter pelts, and he put them at his feet...he continued, naming [Alonso] Torres; he gave him a pelt and another to each of the four of us who were guests; Next he let it be known that we had surprised him without pelts and that therefore he had not given any to the other chiefs, since he had even torn apart one of his own capes: He asked for nothing since the other day he was sent a sumptuous present of copper, hatchets, abalone shells, etc.

Salamanca further reported that on stormy nights the Nootkans would either stay to sleep at the establishment or aboard, or they would ask for a lantern in order to light their way to their village and return it punctually the next day, just as they had done when on other occasions they had asked for copper and hatchets to go to trade with the Nuchimases, and when they returned they paid in pelts which they brought back, such as had been the case with Natzape when he lost them in the canals. A final disconnected statement was that the Nootkans used the latrines aboard with neatness.[7]

Another story related by Salamanca was:

One day when we went to Maquinna's house, he had a banquet in our honour with there being evident on the faces of each one of those of his family the pleasure and gratitude that they had. They put down new mats for us to sit on. They gave us a salmon which were still scarce (it is of the previous year and they conserve it with continuous smoke without salt or any other assistance) and it was the only one which we saw on this occasion. His people roasted it over the coals with great cleanliness so it would not be repugnant to us, and we ate it there with Maquinna and his wives. He was pleased by this frankness and insisted that we eat, pointing out that he ate daily with us whatever we gave him (he excused himself for having neither spoons nor forks, telling everyone that he was very poor); he showed us several pieces of whale meat which he did not serve, giving us to understand by signs that it would turn our stomachs. We were totally unarmed (his wives were aboard our vessels, with both parties unaware of these reciprocal hostages) and both so much without suspicion and happy just like true friends. This house was provisional and just finished in order to be close to us and painted outside in imitation of the poop of a frigate.[8]

While at Nootka the schooners obtained supplies from Captain Bodega y Quadra, made needed repairs, added several crew members to each vessel and acquired a longboat to assist in their operations. Artist Cardero had time to draw a "View of the Bay of Nutca, from the beach of the Spanish settlement," one which shows six Spanish

According to native accounts, Maquinna would close himself in this box when he sought communion with the supernatural. Ink and wash drawing by José Cardero. (Museo Naval 2948; Sotos 652)

vessels, a launch and various native canoes. Probably another of his drawings, "Caxon donde entra el Gefe de Nutka a sus supersticiones," a prayer room or box, was drawn at about the same time in 1792. This oratory occupied a place of honour in Maquinna's home and was described as two metres long and half a metre wide. On the inside there was a grotesque figure "with a most hideous human face, enormously large arms, nails like an eagle's talons, and feet like those of a bear." Its uniqueness induced the explorers to include the drawing done by José Cardero with the other pictures to illustrate the account of the voyage.

The subsequent circumnavigation of Vancouver Island, a laborious task, consumed four full months. Small vessels with poor sailing characteristics, limited crews and inadequate space resulted in minimum attention to journal entries.[9]

On 3 June the explorers made a false start, but were foiled by contrary weather. Maquinna, using Nootkan with appropriate gestures, offered his services to assist them in selecting a proper time of departure, which intervention was accepted by Alcalá Galiano and Valdés, confident that ocean-oriented natives such as the Nootkans would know the proper signs of nature. Instead, the chief prayed to the native deity Cuautle, using Bodega's great house as his place of prayer. Maquinna's intonations, grimaces and gestures were a source of amusement to the Spaniards, but not to his commoners, who listened to him with the greatest reverence. By the afternoon of 4 June, the weather having cleared, the schooners headed toward their first objective, the recently founded Spanish settlement of Núñez Gaona at what is now Neah Bay on the Angeles Peninsula in today's state of Washington. The port had been named in 1790 in honour of Admiral Manuel Núñez Gaona of the Spanish navy. A settlement had been established there in late May 1792 under command of Salvador Fidalgo as a fall back position for Spanish interests in case Spain was forced to cede Nootka to the British. The usefulness of Núñez Gaona was early questioned, since its exposed position made it difficult in the winter months. Viceroy Revilla Gigedo was mixed in his opinion concerning the area, motivated by changing objectives and strategies concerning the northwest. Fidalgo was high on the port, indicating that it "was very fertile, beautiful, healthful and its location very advantageous since no vessel could enter or leave the strait [of Juan de Fuca] without being seen." After his arrival, Fidalgo ordered the construction of a barracks, a bakery with its oven, a blacksmith shop and corrals for the cattle, sheep, goats and pigs that he had imported. Emulating Alberni at Nootka, he began cultivation of a vegetable garden.

Others did not share Fidalgo's opinion concerning Núñez Gaona, including Alcalá Galiano and Valdés, who recommended against it since it would only become an added expense and would be wasted effort. The two visitors told Fidalgo of their recommendation, despite their expressed opinion that the area appeared to be more fertile, have a better climate and more pleasant surroundings than Nootka.

Fidalgo had established favourable rapport with the local natives. Their language was similar to the Nootkans', as were their customs in general, but they were taller, more robust and better formed. With "better shaped" faces, there were two women who were almost "white." The dress of the women was characterized as less modest, acting and dressing with great freedom and very little shame. They used grease to brighten their hair, wore decorative bracelets and necklaces, and adorned their ears and noses with pendants, paying much more attention "to extravagant adornment than do the women

of Nootka."

While at Núñez Gaona, the explorers met Tetacu, a visiting Indian from Esquimalt, just west of modern Victoria. An engaging and well-informed native, he was prevailed upon to act as a guide, sailing aboard the *Mexicana*, although his wife, whom the Spaniards were certain was called María, could not be persuaded to join in what must have been a daring action. Before departure, Artist Cardero made probably the only drawing ever done of the post, entitled "View of the Spanish Establishment in the Port of Núñez Gaona and Great Canoe of Tetaku." That chief's canoe appears to be almost identical with the canoe of Tlupananulg of Nootka, drawn in 1791 by Suria. Cardero may have used the Nootkan's great canoe as the model for this drawing. The scene pictures the schooners and the Frigate *Princesa*, and in the background lies the rudimentary Spanish settlement, the first non-Indian settlement in what would later become the northwestern United States.[10] Cardero also made a drawing of Tetacu and his wife. The Atlas of the Voyage of the *Sutil* and *Mexicana* contains two later engravings of the chief and of his wife, taken from these early drawings. It has sometimes been thought that Tetacu was a Makah from the Cape Flattery area, but a more careful reading of the documents definitely establishes him as from Esquimalt, on southeast Vancouver Island, a Straits Salish village.

Tetacu accompanied the visitors on their trip which was made principally along the north shore of the strait, whereas his wives made a slower trip by native craft. The chief was a model passenger and informant. He ate Spanish food with curiosity, imitated the actions of his hosts, drew pictures with pencil for them, and also gave information concerning English and Spanish captains who had been along the coast. He gave news that there were two large vessels inside the strait.

Although identified as an "Indian fortification," the buildings shown are likely the Spanish settlement at Nuñez Gaona under construction, since Alcalá Galiano makes no mention of a stockaded native village. Ink and wash drawing by José Cardero. (Museo de América 2-350; Palau 67,

Tetacu was solicitous concerning the safety of his wives and used the telescope to search for signs of them. He was happy when they finally appeared, following which Tetacu had the Spaniards as his guests ashore. There he showed them "every attention in his power," a signal honour from a greatly feared chief who held the greatest respect and authority in native society.

After a most satisfactory and informative visit with Tetacu, Alcalá Galiano and Valdés headed their schooners toward the San Juan Islands. In this area Cardero drew two Indian canoes, approaching the schooners which are under sail and towing their launches. In the centre of one canoe a native is standing with arms outstretched in the symbolic gesture of friendship so often seen by the visitors. In the background is the dormant volcanic cone of Mount Baker. The schooners were not the first vessels to penetrate the Strait of Juan de Fuca. Two years earlier Manuel Quimper commanding the *Princesa Real* had explored the southern coast of Vancouver Island into the Strait of Juan de Fuca. He took possession several times, and entered the Puerto de Córdoba (Esquimalt Harbour). He had already taken symbolic possession of Núñez Gaona, and he had also performed similar ceremonies at what is now known as Sooke and Royal Roads on the north shore of the strait and at Dungeness on the south shore. His penetration, hurried by the press of time, reached as far as Bellingham Bay, but he did not realize the magnitude of the task which he had left unfinished. His map, drawn by Gonzalo López de Haro, indicates the extent of this first major reconnaissance.

The following year, 1791, two vessels, the *San Carlos* under Ramón Saavedra, and the smaller *Santa Saturnina* under José María Narváez, entered farther into inland waters. The two Spanish vessels made a rendezvous at Puerto de Córdoba and continued exploration.

Tetacu, chief of the entrance of Juan de Fuca. The cloak he wears is made of sea otter skins; his conical woven hat bears designs depicting a whale hunt. Ink and wash drawing by José Cardero. (Museo de América 2-276; Palau 72, Sotos 645)

Wife of Tetacu by José Cardero. (Museo de América 2.277; Palau 73, Sotos 641)

The second wife of Tetacu. Her clothing is notable for its intricate woven designs. Refined for an engraving by Fernando Selma, after a sketch by José Cardero. (Museo de América 2-279; Palau 75, Sotos 642)

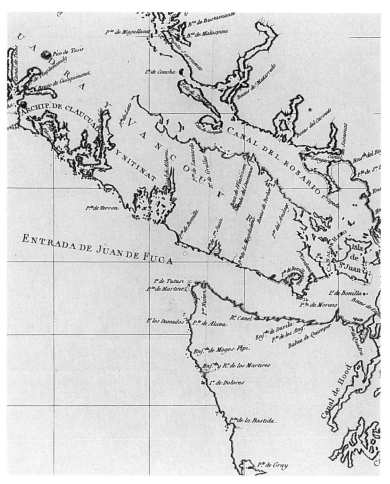

Detail of the chart from the 1792 voyage of the Sutil *and* Mexicana, *showing Spanish place names in modern-day British Columbia and Washington State. (Special Collections, Library, University of British Columbia)*

They chose not to go southward, which would have led them to discovery of Puget Sound, but rather concentrated on exploration to the north. Among their explorations were the San Juan Islands, Rosario Strait, Burrard Inlet and Nanaimo Harbour. The result of their explorations was to leave a map, lacking some detail, but indicating visual contact extending as far north as Powell River, Texada Island and the Courtenay-Comox area. In fact, when Vancouver in 1792 learned of the 1791 activities of the Spanish explorers, he was quite disappointed, realizing that he had been preceded by official Spanish naval exploration into the interior. Alcalá Galiano and Valdés had available a knowledge of these two earlier expeditions, with the result that they used the place names of earlier date in dealing with much of the first part of their exploration.

The 1792 visitors liberally spread new place names on the map, ones which for the most part were not destined to have great longevity, but offer a litany of Malaspina expedition members whom they wished to honour, supplemented by names commemorating leading Spanish naval figures of their day. A few deserving bureaucrats, particularly those who had in some way aided either the Malaspina group or the *Sutil* and *Mexicana*, had their names placed on the "Carta Esférica de los Reconocimientos...." Even members of the schooners' complement were recognized.

Traditional use of religious names, particularly those of favourite saints, so well established in Spanish exploration and place name geography, is almost totally absent. Lack of a priest as chaplain and diarist may have had something to do with this deviation. Occasionally, instead, an event of interest or importance resulted in a place name. Bocas, brazos, calas, puertos, ensenadas, canales, entradas, puntas, islas and archipelagos received a new baptism, with only

The Sutil *and* Mexicana *under sail in the San Juan Islands, with the volcanic cone of Mount Baker showing clearly on the horizon. In the bow of the canoe at the right rests a spear used for hunting seals or sea otters.*

Pen and ink wash drawing by José Cardero. (Museo Naval MS 1723-9; Higueras 2942, Sotos 634)

Portrait of Alcalá Galiano (1760-1805), miniature on paper, anonymous. (Museo Naval A-1365; Higueras 3253)

Cayetano Valdés (1767-1839) was only 25 years old when he was appointed by Malaspina to command the Mexicana. *Being the nephew of Antonio Valdés, Spain's navy minister, likely helped his advancement. From an oil painting by José Roldan. (Museo Naval A-676; Higueras 3250)*

occasional attempts at conservation of aboriginal names. Many place names, no matter what the reason for inclusion, were erased by similar English efforts, by passage of time and by the imminent Spanish disappearance from the Pacific Northwest.

The voyage of the *Sutil* and *Mexicana* is recorded in the written accounts supported or modified by other contemporary sources. Unfortunately, what the local Indians felt about this and other expeditions is impossible to determine except as the information is filtered through non-Indian recorders or has become part of oral tradition of long standing. An extract of the diary dated 23 October 1793 at Monterey in California, and signed by both Alcalá Galiano and Valdés, in about 6500 words treats what the co-commanders thought to be the highlights of the reconnaissance. It is interesting to compare this with the actual diary to determine what the commanding officers felt was most important, or what additions were made. Dealings with Vancouver and his men and difficulties of navigation through the narrow passages, whirlpools and eddies of the most easterly possible passage headed toward the sea, claimed much of the space in the extract, whereas, the time dealing with Vancouver is not treated extensively in the full diary. Even the full diary, as turned in to the Viceroy in Mexico City, was abbreviated from the comments that had been recorded earlier.

Certain portions of the combined diary and extract are salient. Following the description and evaluation of the fledgling settlement at the Port of Núñez Gaona, a second section concerns the intelligence obtained from Tetacu that there were other vessels in the interior, which were immediately thought to be British, a supposition which later proved correct. A third involves the decision not to explore to the south, which would have led to Puget Sound, but rather to concentrate on northern exploration. This was not done with any knowledge of British activity, but rather from the likelihood that any strait seemed more logically to be found toward the north.

Shortly after entering the Gran Canal de Nuestra Señora del Rosario, now known as the Strait of Georgia, the Spaniards sighted the sails of two vessels, but it was not until 13 June that actual contact was made. Lieutenant William R. Broughton of the brigantine *Chatham* boarded the *Sutil* to salute Alcalá Galiano in the name of George Vancouver, and to make known to the Spanish officer the pleasure that the English captain would have in helping the schooners if anything were needed. The Spanish commander thanked Broughton, but indicated that due to contrary winds the schooners could not take advantage at that moment of the offer. Alcalá Galiano said that he was equally at the disposition of the British and conveyed the message that the Spaniards already knew about the resources of the area, indicating that a Spanish vessel had been there a year earlier.

The *Sutil* and *Mexicana* continued eastward, and on 19 and 20 June the two schooners stood off today's city of Vancouver. The explorers had two visits from native small craft, and, probably on the second day, a portrait was done of the Indian Chief of Lángara Point (identified as Point Grey). Four canoes approached, similar to the seven of the previous day. In the largest canoe came an old man of noteworthy seriousness, who seemed to be the chief. He was not impressed by the Spanish presents of beads but was willing to trade a canoe for some small sheets of copper. Upon being invited, the chief came aboard immediately, showing frankness and confidence.

Next, the Spaniards moved westward across the Strait of Georgia, where three drawings were made by Cardero. These were: "Chief of the Wentuisen Entrance" (today's Nanaimo, but then named in honour of Admiral Francisco Xavier Winthuysen, a Spanish officer of Flemish origin); "Chief of the Port of Descanso" (Descanso Bay on Gabriola Island); and a "View of a Natural Gallery on the Northwest Coast of America." The third drawing has been ascribed to other areas and to other artists, but more recent investigation has clearly established it as being on Gabriola Island, though in reality the gallery or corridor is not as impressive as in the drawing done by Cardero, and later finished for engraving by other hands.

The small Spanish schooners returned to the mainland side of the Strait of Georgia, but it was not until 27 June that they met again the English, when early in the morning Captain George Vancouver in a small boat came alongside the *Sutil*. Vancouver was in the area making explorations prior to a meeting that was expected between him and Spanish naval officer Bodega y Quadra, the purpose of which was to consummate the Nootka Sound controversy. Vancouver had with him the recently completed plans of the Canals of Floridablanca, Carmelo and Moniño (which he called Burrard Inlet, Howe Sound and Agamemnon Channel), and he also provided information of the British exploration of the Boca de Caamaño (Puget Sound). According to the Spanish journal, Vancouver offered to furnish any information relative to his explorations, while at the same time renewing his strong suggestion that the Spanish vessels join him in order to be able to work together. This latter invitation does not accord with other sources which indicate that it was Alcalá Galiano who had initiated the idea of joint cooperation. Whatever the truth may be, the Spaniards showed Vancouver the maps that they had, and the two small task groups joined forces for some time.

There is indication of most cordial promises of cooperation on both sides, though the extract indicates that the Spaniards had some

The chief of Descanso Bay on Gabriola Island. Ink and wash drawing by José Cardero. (Museo de América 2-281; Palau 77, Sotos 648)

misgivings in finding themselves working together with men who had better means, particularly in the small boats available. However, the Spanish journalist indicated that the idea of operating together might make the work more useful to European knowledge, a pleasing idea. Furthermore, it was felt that they might learn something about the true object of the British exploration and gain knowledge of their working methods. Subsequent days were filled with friendly cooperation, including several dinners aboard the Spanish and British vessels. It was clear that the British were in a position to advance the exploratory cause more rapidly than the Spaniards, though there is no reason to believe that there was any disparity in the quality of their explorations.

After a fortnight of cooperative activity, on 13 July the two parties split. The British group was motivated by having found what was clearly the most rapid exit toward the Pacific. By following what was to be called Discovery Passage, the distance was greatly shorter than the route followed by the *Sutil* and *Mexicana*. Neither route was easy, but relatively speaking, the Spanish choice was much the more difficult, something already known to Alcalá Galiano and Valdés. A conviction that only by going to the north and east could they fulfill their instructions led the Spaniards to separate after cooperation that had been "not only harmonious, but also of the closest friendship." As a parting gesture the British and Spanish commanders exchanged copies of their surveys.

The route chosen by the Spaniards, the one which would carry the schooners as close to the mainland as possible in their search for the strait, let them immediately into the Angostura de los Comandantes (Arran Rapids). Both the British and the local Indians warned the Spanish explorers of the potential danger, peril from which the

The Coast Salish chief of Langara Point, identified as present-day Point Grey (in Vancouver, British Columbia), near where the Spanish expedition met Captain Vancouver's ships Discovery *and* Chatham. *Ink and wash drawing by José Cardero. (Museo Naval MS 1725-5-2; Higueras 2946, Sotos 649)*

The chief of Wentuisen Harbour, present-day Nanaimo, encountered by Alcalá Galiano and Valdés. Ink and wash drawing by José Cardero. (Museo Naval MS 1725-5.1; Higueras 2947, Sotos 647)

Spaniards narrowly escaped on several occasions. The schooners, certainly more by luck than by knowledge of the dangers, made their way through the eddies, whirlpools and rapids that lay before them. The extract likens the Narrows of the Commandants to the Angostura de la Esperanza in the Strait of Magellan, save for the fact that the estimate of current velocity of twelve knots was greater in their existing circumstances by about four knots. Passage through the dangerous passage was facilitated by considerable help and plentiful advice from local Indians.

The decision to keep close to the mainland led the Spaniards to explorations of coastal inlets, as well as to long hours at the oars in small boat explorations. Such exertions made occasional days of rest necessary, but even these were filled with activity and concern.

Cardero's drawings add visual dimension to the route chosen by Alcalá Galiano and Valdés even prior to final separation from Vancouver's vessels. During a small boat reconnaissance into what is today called Toba Inlet, the party led by Cayetano Valdés found an interesting wooden plank on a hill on the east side of the inlet. On it there were various hieroglyphics, and Valdés made a sketch of them, which in turn were converted into a drawing by José Cardero. From this find the inlet gained the temporary name of Canal de la Tabla. A short time later it received the name of the Brazo de Toba, in honor of Antonio de Tova Arredondo, second in command of the *Atrevida*.

Cardero next drew a view of the "End of Salamanca Channel and a Suspicious Following by the Indians" showing a launch being followed by numerous Kwakiutl Indian canoes. The scene results from native misgivings concerning the intentions of the visitors. Later Brambila did an "improved version" of this scene, into which he introduced a two-man kayak, and to which he added an unbelievable

A wooden plank bearing "hieroglyphics" was found on the eastern shore of Toba Inlet by a crew led by Cayetano Valdés. Drawing by José Cardero from a sketch by Valdés. (Museo de América 2.275; Palau 71, Sotos 651)

Lieutenant Secundino Salamanca exploring in a launch at the head of the inlet that the Spanish named after him, later renamed Loughborough Inlet by the British. The Spanish were nervous at the massed approach of canoes, but the natives left without incident. Pencil, ink and wash drawing by José Cardero. (Museo Naval MS 1723-22; Higueras 2943, Sotos 637)

This unusual eroded rock formation on Gabriola Island is still known as Malaspina Gallery. Drawing perhaps by Fernando Brambila, from a sketch by José Cardero. (Museo de América 2.273; Palau 69, Sotos 555)

number of native craft, since Cardero had perhaps already overemphasized the danger when he drew many in the original scene. Salamanca's name was given to the channel which today is called Loughborough Inlet.

Subsequently, Juan Vernacci set out on another sortie to explore what was at that time given the name Vernacci Channel, but is today Knight Inlet. Apparently Cardero accompanied this six-day trip and drew a "View of Bernaci Channel and a Great Waterfall," that showed an exceedingly great thrust of water emitting from the hillside. Three canoes of Kwakiutl Indians are seen, in one of which a chief is standing with his arms extended in the sign of peace. In the launch, a Spaniard is standing with something in his hands, which has led to the guess that this was the artist engaged in drawing the scene. Another possibility is that it was an officer or pilot engaged in taking bearings or making a rudimentary chart.

In general, dealings with the local natives were good, but one incident, late in the circumnavigation, probably in the vicinity of Cracroft Island, caused a period of uneasiness aboard the schooners. While Lieutenant Vernacci was away exploring the channel to which his name was given, a small detachment of six men from the *Sutil* went ashore to cut wood. Formerly friendly Indians became belligerent when their efforts at obtaining guns in trade were rejected. Seeing that this was refused, three of them advanced on one man to take away the gun in his hand, but other Spaniards came to his aid and forced the Indians to embark in their canoes. In a small boat, Salamanca came to the reenforcement of the party.

A cannon shot without ball was immediately fired from on board and produced the expected effect. As soon as Salamanca found that nothing

A chief from the north end of Vancouver Island, in what is now Kwagiulth territory, wears a headdress and ear pendants and has decorated his face and body with paint. Ink and wash drawing by José Cardero. (Museo de América 2-282; Palau 78, Sotos 650)

Coastal surveys were mostly undertaken in small boats commanded by ships' officers. Here Juan Vernacci explores what the Spanish called "Canal de Vernacci," now Knight Inlet. Ink and wash drawing by José Cardero. (*Museo de América 2-341; Palau 79, Sotos 636*)

The Sutil *and* Mexicana *at anchor off a large native village they called "Maguaa" or "Majoa" after its chief. Its location on the expedition's map is vague, but it may be on Vancouver Island, across from the southern end of Malcolm Island, today an Indian reserve. Ink and wash drawing by José Cardero. (Museo de América 2-280; Palau 76, Sotos 639)*

had happened to our men and nothing had been stolen from them he refrained from pursuing the fugitives, who had stopped a short distance away with their paddles raised. In order to make them understand that they were not yet safe and what were the kind of enemies they were looking for, a cannon ball was fired with some elevation. Passing over their heads, as was desired, it fell on to the ground much beyond where they were. This frightened them very much, if one could judge from the rate of paddling at which they retired. They reached their settlement where there was a great shouting, but seeing that we not only were not coming to it but kept on with our cutting of wood and went ashore to make observations, they quieted down. In the future there was no more disturbance, nor did they come alongside.[11]

In writing to the viceroy, the commanders indicated that this "has been the only trouble we have had in the whole campaign, and brought us the satisfaction of seeing that our men, possessed by the spirit of humanity with which we had endeavoured to imbue them, contented themselves with beating them, although attacked by such a large number."[12]

In subsequent days, Cardero made two additional drawings which represent the itinerary of the expedition. A "View of the Great Rancheria of Maguaa [Majoa]" was done of the large village on the south shore of Johnstone Strait. Indian canoes abound. In the foreground a Kwakiutl chief, bedecked in furs, is being transported in a canoe by four local natives. This was done about 9 August, shortly after the schooners had had contact with the *Venus*, a British trading ship out of Bengal, Henry Shepherd commanding.

Cardero's final drawing during the circumnavigation was of an "Indian of the Northwest Coast at the Salida de las Goletas [Goletas Channel]." There is no mention of the specific circumstances of this portraiture, but since considerable time was spent at Port Guemes

(today, Port Hardy), so called in honour of one of the family names of the viceroy who was patron of the expedition, it is quite possible that this Kwakiutl native was from that area.

Having made celestial observations for regulating the marine chronometers and locating precisely the mouth of the Canal de la Salida, the schooners attempted to seek shelter at what was perhaps Shushartie Bay, awaiting a favourable northwest wind, but circumstances did not permit. Rather they made their way southeast along the coast to a familiar location, Point Boiset (or Frondoso), later called Cape Cook, not far from Nootka.

Upon arrival at Nootka, thereby completing the first full continuous circumnavigation of what at that time was called Vancouver and Quadra's Island, the schooners stopped briefly at the Spanish port. They arrived 31 August, to find that the British vessels *Discovery* and *Chatham* had arrived a few days earlier, with the latter undergoing repairs. The *Sutil* and *Mexicana* were boot-topped on 1 September to clear their bottoms, and by just after midnight they were under way, bound for Monterey and San Blas.[13]

Epilogue

As far as anyone in that area knew when Malaspina left the Pacific Northwest in 1791, little had been decided about international rights concerning limits of influence, nor had a definitive conclusion been reached about the existence of the storied Strait of Ferrer Maldonado. A year later when his sub-expedition departed under Alcalá Galiano and Valdés, the Nootka Sound Controversy was still unresolved, though things did not look good for Spain. The idea of a potential dividing line between Spanish interests and those of the other powers was under consideration as a result of Juan de la Bodega y Quadra's Expedition of the Limits to the North of California. Fruitless search for the fabled strait had been augmented by the combined and occasionally coordinated efforts of Alcalá Galiano and Valdés on one side and of Vancouver on the other.

In both 1791 and 1792 the Spanish explorers, after protracted exploration in northern waters, went south to the more benign area of California. Neither time did they carry out a very close reconnaissance of the intervening coast, probably feeling that many other expeditions had passed that way and that they could hardly add more to the record. Monterey became a rest stop both times, permitting the tired crews such recuperation as the California capital was capable of providing before they returned to the insalubrious tropical climes of Acapulco or San Blas. Despite the need for recuperation, the stopovers were hardly days of idleness, for time was spent in adding to collections and gathering new information, as well as finalizing the papers concerning activity farther north, an ordering of notes and charts that was not easily done at sea.

On first glance it seems remarkable that Malaspina and his groups did not have a greater impact on the places they visited. This could be excused concerning Mulgrave where there were no local recorders of such a stay, but at Nootka the reports of Spanish sources there have very little to say concerning the visits of the *Descubierta* and *Atrevida* and of the *Sutil* and *Mexicana*, and from California it is the same. There are merely terse comments concerning what was Spain's major contribution to eighteenth-century natural science. The answer, as has been previously indicated, is simple – Malaspina and his groups were visiting precisely for the purpose of reporting directly to the court. It probably never entered into the minds of those at Nootka that they should make even a minimal report on a senior officer or his efforts other than merely to acknowledge officially the presence of the distinguished visitors. After all, Malaspina and Bustamante out-ranked anyone in the areas involved. They might ask local officers for reports to aid in their research, but they would hardly be the subject of reports originating from their juniors.

In neither the archives of California nor the correspondence emanating from the senior commander at Nootka is there much help in attempting to determine the impact of the scientists' visit. There is more locally generated documentation for the 1792 visit since one of the chief reasons for Bodega's presence at Nootka was to lend all possible support to the operations being carried out by the schooners *Sutil* and *Mexicana*. Even so, there is very little available information beyond that reported by the commanders of those little vessels.

The itinerary of the rest of the Malaspina main group took it across the Pacific after staging for that new operation at Acapulco. There, some members joined the expedition for the first time. Detached parties which had been on junkets in Mexico rejoined the vessels, and a sizeable number were permanently detached from the main party to join the *Sutil* and *Mexicana* or to depart for other destinations. Malaspina's party made visits to Guam, the Philippines, Macao, Australia, New Zealand and several island groups of Oceania. The four years originally planned for the cruise lengthened into a little over five years, partly due to the Northwest Coast detour and also due to the need on return to join as part of trans-Atlantic convoy for protection against feared enemy vessels, as a result of general European hostilities.

Following return to Spain, Malaspina was feted, promoted[1] and given a free hand in readying for publication the chief results of the expedition. Bustamante soon returned to typical senior officer duties. It was clear that Malaspina was considered the heart of the now completed expedition. He was able to obtain the services of Alcalá Galiano and Cardero, and all were in Madrid working together on the final report.

For reasons not fully clear, Malaspina became the target of royal disfavour, egged on by Chief of State Manuel Godoy. Certainly, Malaspina's fall from grace was in some way associated with his liberal political ideas and his popularity as a returned hero, and complicated greatly by his political inexperience. Malaspina was clearly beyond his capacity in Spanish politics of the last decade of the eighteenth century.

Unfortunately, Malaspina and his expedition could no longer count on the aid and intervention of long-time champion Antonio Valdés y Bazán, who had been relieved of duty as minister of the navy. Different explanations have been offered at various times to explain Malaspina's loss of favour. Some have thought that there was a carefully orchestrated rivalry between Malaspina and Godoy, with Queen María Luisa de Parma being the object of these hostile feelings. This gives a melodramatic, but a not entirely plausible, twist to Malaspina's downfall. It has been further suggested that certain persons in high places sought to replace Godoy in the queen's special favour with the heroic mariner from the same duchy as the queen.

Other explanations involve Malaspina's ideas of opening limited free trade as a solution for regeneration of a decaying colonial empire that was becoming increasingly the target of clandestine commerce. Some even feel that Malaspina fostered a commonwealth arrangement for a vast overseas empire which was clearly on the brink of disaster. Any and all of these ideas were repugnant to Carlos IV and his son (later Fernando VII), who were attempting to consolidate absolute monarchy in an age when constitutionalism was in the ascendancy.

Whatever the true causes, Malaspina was taken prisoner by night, searched and whisked off to jail. After his state trial in which he was found guilty, on 17 April 1796 he was stripped of his newly obtained commission as commodore. In accordance with the sentence of his court martial, Malaspina was sent to a prison in the gloomy fortress of San Antón in La Coruña, Galicia. There he languished, whether actually in a cell or under the more gentlemanly status of house arrest is uncertain, until 1802. At that date, after more than six years at San Antón, his sentence was commuted to that of banishment to his native Duchy of Parma on pain of death if ever he were to return to Spain. Scant documentation sheds almost no light on his last years save for the information that he was engaged in some minor governmental activity. Malaspina died in the house of a prosperous dry goods dyer in Pontremoli on 9 April 1810.

Little trace resulted, except for scattered place names, of Malaspina's grand expedition. As for the two corvettes, the *Descubierta* and *Atrevida*, which had been constructed with such high hopes of Spain surpassing with them the scientific achievements of Captain Cook, they were soon refitted and assigned to normal line duty. The end came for the *Atrevida* in 1807 in Montevideo, the very port of its first visit, when the twenty-gun corvette caught fire and burned while under the command of Don Antonio de Ibarra. The *Descubierta* finally passed from active service as a nearly forty-year-old corvette when it was sold at Cádiz by royal order in 1828. The purchaser was one Don Felipe Biera who bought it for 151,011 *reales vellón*. To what use it was placed at that time has not yet been discovered.

Bustamante enjoyed a successful career after conclusion of the expedition but never was involved in any follow-up aspects of that lengthy cruise. He was rewarded by promotion to rear admiral and returned to routine naval duty. His later life is illustrative of his evident merit, with service from 1797 to 1804 as governor of Uruguay (an area that had been visited by the expedition in 1789), from 1810 to 1819 as captain general of Guatemala during the Latin American Wars for Independence and finally as director general of the Spanish navy. All of these commands were superior to any that Malaspina received as his reward for participation in the exploratory expedition. Bustamante outlived Malaspina by fifteen years, though he was only four years younger than his friend and colleague. He died in Madrid in 1825.

The commanders of the sloops *Sutil* and *Mexicana* also benefited from the promotions they received while with Malaspina and from the relatively high position that they achieved early in life. Dionisio Alcalá Galiano had a brief but brilliant career, cut short by his martyr's death as one of Spain's naval heroes of the Battle of Trafalgar. During that great naval engagement off the south coast of Spain, he was decapitated by a cannon shot while commanding the warship *Bahama*. His comrade of 1792, Cayetano Valdés, lived a long life, one filled with military action and honours, including participation in the battle off Cape Trafalgar. He participated in political movements and was involved at the highest levels of government. Imprisoned for several years in the Castle of Santa Bárbara in Alicante as a subversive, he subsequently spent long years of exile in England, followed by restoration to the highest levels of military command, and final burial in the Pantheon of Illustrious Mariners.

Malaspina, beyond a promotion immediately after return from the long cruise, gained nothing. He suffered what was probably the cruelest fate, that of being forgotten. Even his name was prohibited from being mentioned in connection with the round-the-world cruise to which he had dedicated so much of his career. Officially he became a non-person, and the project to which he had dedicated so much failed to find any significant publication during his lifetime and for many years thereafter. He lost his military rank with its advantages, his reputation and his freedom, with the result that the fruits of his scientific labour were nearly lost completely.

Notes

1 Donald C. Cutter (ed.), *Journal of Tomás de Suria and His Voyage with Malaspina to the Northwest Coast of America in 1791* (Fairfield, Washington, 1980), pp. 35-6, (hereinafter cited as Suria, *Voyage*).

2 George Dixon, *A Voyage round the world, but more particularly to the Northwest Coast of America* (London, 1789). Dixon, a veteran of Captain James Cook's third and last great expedition, had later returned to the coast as a merchant mariner in the service of the King George's Sound Company.

3 Donald C. Cutter, *Malaspina in California* (San Francisco, 1960), p. 1.

4 A paper which had much influence was "Memoria sobre el descubrimiento del Paso del Noroeste o del Mar Oceano al del Sur por la parte septentrional de la América leida en la Real Academia de Ciencias de Paris por M. Buache, Geógrafo Mayor de S.M. Cristianísimo." The author of the paper was Philippe Buache de Neuville, a prominent French geographer of the last half of the eighteenth century.

5 Late eighteenth-century Spanish sailing in the North Pacific used San Blas as the prime meridian.

6 This document, signed on 15 April 1791 at San Blas by Juan Francisco de la Bodega y Quadra, is in Costa N.O. de América, tomo II, MS 332 in Museo Naval.

7 Alejandro Malaspina, *Viaje científico y político a la América Meridional, a las Costas del Mar Pacífico y a las Islas Marianas y Filipinas verificado en los años de 1789, 90, 91, 92, 93 y 94 a bordo de las corbetas Descubierta y Atrevida de la Marina Real, mandadas por los capitanes de navío D. Alejandro Malaspina y D. José F. Bustamante* (Madrid, 1984), pp. 220-22. This is a substantial reproduction of Pedro de Novo y Colson's edition of the same material edited in 1885.

8 Instrucción que el Exmo. Señor Virey [Revilla Gigedo] dió a los comandantes de los Buques de exploraciones in California, Historia y Viajes, tomo I, MS 575 in Museo Naval.

9 Suria, *Voyage*, p. 28.

10 Lorenzo San Feliu Ortiz (ed.), *62 Meses a bordo: La Expedición Malaspina según el diario del Teniente de Navéo Don Antonio de Tova Arredondo, 2° Comandante de la ATREVIDA, 1789-1794 (Madrid 1943), pp. 138-39.*

11 Bauzá was born in the Balaeric Islands, and prior to the Malaspina cruise held the post of teacher of drawing and fortifications at the Spanish Midshipmen's School at Cádiz. In later years he became custodian of much of the cartography and some of the art emanating from the sixty-two-month voyage of the corvettes. He spent much of his later life as an exile, living in England and having with him some materials related to the expedition. Although he planned to return to Spain, he died on 8 April 1834 at age 70 at Johnson Street, Somerstown. The ceremony of burial was performed by Joseph Kimbell, chaplain of the Catholic Chapel, Moorfields, in the Parish of St. Stephen, Coleman Street, London. His last will had been made many years earlier in Gibraltar on 22 October 1823. Partida de Defunción y Testamento de Bauzá, MS 1821 in Museo Naval. A series of thirty-three coastal views drawn by Bauzá while on the Northwest Coast, now in the Museo Naval, can be used to trace the approximate route of the corvettes, especially in the more northerly areas.

12 For example, while in San Blas the observatory was established in the home of Captain Bodega, commandant of the naval department. In Monterey, a portion of the Presidio was set aside for scientific uses, while at Nootka the tents were set up very close to the houses of the Spanish establishment.

13 Details of the Bohemian savant's life are found in Laurio H. Destefani and Donald Cutter, *Tadeo Haenke y el final de una vieja polémica* (Buenos Aires, 1966).

14 We know very little of the circumstances of such unofficial collections as he made, but we do have knowledge of the eventual disposition of some of the materials which he collected while on the Northwest Coast. They are in the Náprstek Museum which forms part of the National Museum of Czechoslovakia in Prague, some items of which are included here as illustrations. A listing of these surviving items is in Joseph Kandert, "Catalogue of Ethnographical Collections of Tadéas Hanke," in *Annals of the Náprstek Museum 13* (Prague, 1985), pp. 201-15. For the most part they are repetitive of things which made up the expedition collection. How these pieces arrived in Central Europe is not clear. They may have been sent there after return of the corvettes to Acapulco following the Northwest Coast phase of the great voyage. Tadeo Haenke, one of the most interesting and versatile members of the group, stayed with the major expedition in its round trip across the Pacific Ocean, following which he was "temporarily detached" at Callao, Peru, to continue his researches in the interior of South

15 Donald C. Cutter, "Las Dotaciones y la travesía," in *La Expedición Malaspina, 1789-1794: Viaje a América y Oceania de las Corbetas "Descubierta" y "Atrevida"* (Madrid, 1984), pp. CXLII-CXLVIII. Although their names may have been altered in Spanish orthography, the following were listed as being deserters of the French expedition of Lapérouse: Luis Sereno, Alejo Fuerte and Jean Choli. It also seems likely that another crew member, Pedro Choli, had been with that French expedition. A note by his name indicates that he did not know Spanish. A reasonable assumption is that he and Jean Choli were relatives.

America, with the planned objective of rejoining the corvettes months later in Buenos Aires. He went to numerous places, remitted various reports, and collected his salary for many years until death overtook him in 1817 in Cochabamba, Bolivia, the result of accidental poisoning. He always considered himself as a member of the Spanish Scientific Exploring Expedition and any collections he made logically belonged to the government that was paying him. He may have carried the Northwest Coast specimens with him on his long and often painful trip to Cochabamba, but it seems unlikely. The best guess is that he sent these personal materials either from Acapulco or from Callao as part of his private possessions.

16 Malaspina, *Viaje científico y político...*, p. 223.

17 Some personnel deserted, stayed away for a while, and later rejoined the expedition vessels, either voluntarily or after being apprehended by local authorities.

18 In the previously noted absence of Chief of Natural History Pineda, his role was partly filled by Dr. González of the *Atrevida*. The doctor's observations while on the Northwest Coast are contained in the Chief's notes in his "Descripciones del Sr. Gonzales hechas en el Viage a los 60 [degrees] N." in Pineda, Notas, consisting of two legajos in the Archivo del Museo de Ciencias Naturales in Madrid. While at Mulgrave, González became fascinated with the unusual characteristics of sea otter kidneys, which he described in a brief entry entitled "Diseccion Anathomica de una Nutria que se adquirio en el Puerto de Mulgrave," concerning which he added: "I had Pepe [Cardero] paint it because it seemed to me very worthy of being illustrated in its natural state; I don't know where the painting is." The coloured drawing became part of the expedition pictorial archive and is now in the Museo Naval in Madrid.

19 *Tratado de las enfermedades de la gente de mar, en que se exponen sus causas y los medios de precaverlas* (Madrid, 1805).

20 Casks were treated by various means. They should never have been used for any other type of liquid, and had to be scrubbed completely, following which the casks were treated with sulphur or other additives.

21 On 14 July 1775, a seven-man working party sent ashore from the *Sonora* for water and poles was attacked by the Indians. All hands were lost. See: Herbert K. Beals, trans. & ed., *For Honor & Country: The Diary of Bruno De Hezeta* (Portland, 1985), pp. 77-8.

22 Suria, *Voyage*, p. 30.

23 Suria, *Voyage*, p. 50.

24 Suria, *Voyage*, pp. 28-9.

25 Tova, *62 Meses a bordo*, p. 139.

26 Tova, *62 Meses a bordo*, p. 139.

27 Malaspina, *Viaje científico y político...*, p. 228.

28 Tova, *62 Meses a bordo,* 138.

29 Suria, *Voyage*, p. 33.

30 Suria, *Voyage*, p. 33.

31 Tova, *62 Meses a bordo*, pp. 140-41.

32 Tova, *62 Meses a bordo*, p. 141.

33 Suria, *Voyage*, p. 34.

34 Suria, *Voyage*, pp. 33-4.

35 Tova, *62 Meses a bordo*, p. 142.

36 Suria, *Voyage*, pp. 34-5.

FIRST CONTACT: PORT MULGRAVE

1 Suria, *Voyage*, p. 35.

2 Tova, *62 Meses a bordo*, p. 142.

3 Suria, *Voyage*, pp. 36-7.

4 Suria, *Voyage*, p. 37.

5 Libro de Guardias, Descubierta, MS 729 in Museo Naval.

6 The entire document was written by Malaspina on 28 June and was entered into the Libro de Guardias, Descubierta, MS 729 in Museo Naval.

7 Suria, *Voyage*, p. 37.

8 Tova, *62 Meses a bordo*, p. 143.

9 Tova, *62 Meses a bordo*, pp. 143-44.

10 Tova, *62 Meses a bordo*, p. 144.

11 Malaspina, *Viaje científico y político...*, pp. 238-39.

12 Suria, *Voyage*, p. 37.

13 Suria, *Voyage*, pp. 37-8.

14 Suria, *Voyage*, pp. 37-8.

15 Tova, *62 Meses a bordo*, p. 144.

16 Tova, *62 Meses a bordo*, p. 146.

17 Malaspina, *Viaje científico y político...*, p. 244.

18 Tova, *62 Meses a bordo*, p. 145.

19 Malaspina, *Viaje científico y político...*, pp. 245-46.

20 The Spanish *toesa* is the French *toise*, an ancient, somewhat imprecise measure, based on the maximum extension of the arms sideways from the body. In English it is roughly the fathom. Modern equivalence of the toesa is 6.395 feet and would

make the Spanish measurement of Mt. St. Elias 17,855 feet, a little more than 150 feet short of its modern elevation figure. However, this depends upon the exact measurement of the toesa.

21 Tova, *62 Meses a bordo*, pp. 145-46.

22 Tova, *62 Meses a bordo*, p. 145.

23 Descubierta y Atrevida, Observaciones, MS 264 in Museo Naval.

24 "Maderas de construcción, de fabricas, y muebles...," in Pacífico América, tomo I, f. 257, MS 126 in Museo Naval.

25 Suria, *Voyage*, pp. 48-9.

26 On a separate sheet the following items were written:

taje = mosquito; tge = stone; fato = ice; and thiau = canoe.

27 Suria, *Voyage*, pp. 47-8; Tova, *62 Meses a bordo*, pp. 144-45.

28 Malaspina, *Viaje científico y político...*, p. 249.

29 Tova, *62 Meses a bordo*, p. 147.

30 Malaspina, *Viaje científico y político...*, p. 250.

31 Malaspina, *Viaje científico y político...*, pp. 250-51.

32 Malaspina, *Viaje científico y político...*, p. 251.

33 Tova, *62 Meses a bordo*, p. 149.

34 Malaspina, *Viaje científico y político...*, p. 254.

35 A somewhat variant version of the lost crew member is contained in Suria, *Voyage*, pp. 40-1. Since the artist was not a member of the party, but was telling the story second hand, it seems not to have the same credibility, especially since Suria calls the missing sailor by a different name. "While they were conducting this operation [of possession taking] they missed a sailor, and in searching for him they had to waste all afternoon until they saw him coming, almost dead with cold and totally changed. It happened that on seeing the commander's zeal and desire to find the strait, he went on foot above the Frozen Bay [glacier] to satisfy himself by his own eyes where was the end of the bay. He actually reached the farthest point and saw that it ended in a copious river which ran between those mountains and was lost to view, winding about like a snake. We missed him at midday and he came about 10 o'clock in the afternoon (I call it so because there is no night). According to his account it was a miracle that he had escaped with his life, not only because of the cold but because from one side to the other the sea submerged it and then it froze over again. In view of this feat it will not be thought strange to say that the Spaniards undertake the most arduous enterprises, risking their lives for the honour of their country. It is worth recording his name, José Berelo, a native of La Coruña in the kingdom of Galicia, twenty-eight years of age, of medium though sturdy build." Federica de Laguna, *Under Mount Saint Elias: The History and Culture of the Yakutat Tlingit* (Washington, D.C., 1972), p. 149, suggests that the missing crew member saw Russell Fiord on his unauthorized trip

36 In Acapulco twelve mariners, characterized as among the best of the crew, had deserted. The seeming cause had been an "unfounded fear" of the dangers of the forthcoming Pacific Northwest Coast campaign. The importance of finding them was so great as to cause various efforts in their apprehension, such as sending out parties to apprehend them along the road which it was thought that they would take toward Mexico City and announcing a bounty for any of the local populace who would return them to Acapulco. The second of these methods met with success, the deserters having only gotten some 120 kilometres away from the coast.

37 Tova, *62 Meses a bordo*, pp. 149-50..

38 Malaspina, *Viaje científico y político...*,, pp. 254-55.

39 Tova, *62 Meses a bordo*, p. 152. This incident of thievery is said by Suria, *Voyage*, p. 38 to have taken place on 3 July.

40 Tova, *62 Meses a bordo*, p. 155.

41 Malaspina, *Viaje científico y político...*, p. 247.

42 Malaspina, *Viaje científico y político...*, p. 247.

43 Malaspina, *Viaje científico y político...*, p. 247.

44 Suria, *Voyage*, p. 47.

45 Malaspina, *Viaje científico y político...*, p. 248-49. The pictorial archive of the expedition has three such drawings of the sepulchres. Two are similar and the other quite distinct. Two are obviously done by Cardero and are signed by him.

The third, an "improved copy" done later by Brambila, takes considerable artistic license. All are in the Museo Naval collections. The artistic representation of the winter house without a roof in the Museo de América is signed by José Cardero.

46 Tova, *62 Meses a bordo*, pp. 153-54.

47 Tova, *62 Meses a bordo*, p. 154.

48 Suria, *Voyage*, p. 39.

49 Tova, *62 Meses a bordo*, p. 154.

50 Suria, *Voyage*, p. 41.

51 Tova, *62 Meses a bordo*, p. 155.

52 Suria, *Voyage*, p. 41.

53 This entire confrontation of 5 July was also captured by the drawings of Suria that form an interesting set of illustrations of on-the-scene reporting. Although sketchy, these drawings are perhaps the closest to the true action as it unfolded.

54 Suria, *Voyage*, pp. 41-2.

55 Tova, *62 Meses a bordo*, pp. 156-58. The Spaniards were not able to ascertain the source of Tlingit iron.

56 Suria, *Voyage*, pp. 42-5.

57 Suria, *Voyage*, pp. 45-6.

58 This section in Suria's notebook was followed by seven sketches. Both the quotation and the sketches are in the Yale University manuscript journal of Suria's voyage with Malaspina and are also found in Suria, *Voyage*, p. 49 et passim.

59 Tova, *62 Meses a bordo*, pp. 142, 145.

60 Suria, *Voyage*, p. 39.

61 Elsewhere the spelling in Spanish sources is *chouut*, but seems to be the same word.

62 Malaspina, *Viaje científico y político...*, p. 240.

63 Malaspina, *Viaje científico y político...*, pp. 243-44. There seems to be almost totally missing from the retrievable documentation the results of most of Haenke's efforts at recording native songs. On several occasions there is direct testimony that the Bohemian savant and jack-of-all-trades took the opportunity to copy the native music, but only a few stanzas have come to light.

64 Tova, *62 Meses a bordo,* p. 155-56.

65 Malaspina, *Viaje científico y político...*, p. 248.

66 Ciriaco Cevallos in Libro de Guardias, Atrevida, MS 755 in Museo Naval. Similar sentiments, but less detailed, are found in Tova, *62 Meses a bordo,* p. 156.

67 Suria, *Voyage*, p. 42 and Tova, *62 Meses a bordo,* p. 158.

ALONG THE ALASKA COAST

1 Tova, *62 Meses a bordo,* pp. 159-60.

2 Suria, *Voyage,* p. 51.

3 Suria, *Voyage,* p. 52.

4 Suria, *Voyage,* p. 54.

5 Suria, *Voyage,* p. 54-5.

6 Malaspina, *Viaje científico y político...,* p. 275. Even among members of the expedition, Dionisio Alcalá Galiano was at times referred to as simply Galiano, though improperly. The Northwest Coast remembers him as Galiano though the author calls him by his proper baptismal name – Dionisio Alcalá Galiano y Alcalá Galiano.

7 Suria, *Voyage,* p. 55.

8 Tova, *62 Meses a bordo,* p. 160. To a nearby opening, the delta of the Copper River, the name Valle de Ruesga was given, obviously with some intervention from Tova since that was a transfer name commemorating on the Alaska coast that officer's birth place in northern Spain.

9 Suria, *Voyage,* p. 58.

10 Suria, *Voyage,* p. 58 and Tova, *62 Meses a bordo,* p. 161.

11 Malaspina, *Viaje científico y político...,* p. 283.

12 Tova, *62 Meses a bordo,* p. 161-62.

13 Suria, *Voyage,* pp. 67-8.

14 Suria, *Voyage,* p. 71.

15 Suria, *Voyage,* p. 72.

A VISIT TO NOOTKA

1 Suria, *Voyage,* p. 72.

2 Malaspina, *Viaje científico y político...,* p. 291.

3 Malaspina, *Viaje científico y político...,* pp. 291-92.

4 Suria, *Voyage,* p. 73 and Malaspina, *Viaje científico y político...,* p. 292.

5 Suria, *Voyage,* p. 72.

6 Libro de Guardias, Descubierta, MS 729 in Museo Naval.

7 Suria, *Voyage,* pp. 72-3 and Libro de Guardias, Descubierta, MS 729 in Museo Naval.

8 Mazarredo Island was named for Admiral José de Mazarredo, who has no other connection with the Pacific Northwest. See: Iris H. Wilson [Engstrand] (ed.), *Noticias de Nutka: An Account of Nootka Sound in 1792* (Seattle and London, 1970), p. 3.

9 Libro de Guardias, Descubierta, MS 729 in Museo Naval and Tova, *62 Meses a bordo,* p. 165.

10 Suria, *Voyage,* p. 75.

11 In Malaspina, 1788-1814, MS 2296 in Museo Naval.

12 "Maderas de construcción, de fabricas, y muebles...," in Pacífico América, tomo I, f. 257v, MS 126 in Museo Naval.

13 Suria, *Voyage,* p. 76.

14 Libro de Guardias, Descubierta, MS 729 in Museo Naval.

15 Details of Alberni's agricultural efforts can be found in Donald C. Cutter, "Pedro Alberni y los primeros experimentos de agricultura científica en la costa Noroeste del Pacífico," in *Revista de Historia Naval,* Año V, No. 18 (1987), pp. 41-55.

16 Moachat is the modern preferred usage for what the Spaniards and other early visitors called the Nootkans. However, since the terms Nootkan and Nootka were utilized in the documentary record upon which this study is based, that terminology has been preserved when dealing with the Moachats of past historic times.

17 Malaspina, *Viaje político y científico...*, pp. 362-63. The pagination cited here is from the 1885 edition, since this section was not included in the 1984 edition.

18 Bauzá, Diario al rededor del Mundo, tomo A, MS 479 in Museo Naval.

19 Saavedra's list, dated 21 August 1791, is found in Malaspina Correspondencia, tomo II, MS 279 in Museo Naval.

20 Entry of 26 August 1791 by Jacobo Murphy in Libro de Guardias, Atrevida, MS 755 in Museo Naval.

21 Donald C. Cutter, "The First American in California," in *The Californians,* Vol. 1, No. 5 (September-October 1983), pp. 25-7.

22 This material is part of a large five volume manuscript collection, Costa Oriental de la América Meridional en 1790, tomo V, MS 289 in Museo Naval.

23 Except where the material is in quotations, I have used the most widely accepted English spelling of the Nootka chief's name – Maquinna. The following variants in spelling were found and are listed in alphabetical order with their source in parentheses: Macouina (Roquefeuil); Macquinna (Broughton); Macquinnah (Kendrick deed); Macuina (*62 Meses a bordo*); Macuyna (Noticias de un sacerdote); Makuina (Libro de Guardias); Maquilla (Meares); Maquina (Patterson); Marquirnar (Boaz's Vocabulary); Mocuina (Examen Político); Mokwinna (Moser); Moquina (Ingraham); Moquinna (also Ingraham); Taquina (Libro de Guardias). In all cases the first vowel is an open sound, but its precise value is not easily determined. Almost without exception, the remainder of the word is an attempt to spell what all the visitors heard, and there would be scarcely any difference in the pronunciation except for the case of Meares's Maquilla and the Taquina of the Libro de Guardias.

24 From an untitled box of documents MS 2513 in Museo Naval. This document mentions reserve supplies of clothing, woolens, canvas and stockings for the personnel. In addition, there were two bird whistles, cigarettes, soap, decoys, fishing gear and other equipment.

25 Entry of 15 August in Libro de Guardias, Atrevida, MS 755 in Museo Naval. Variant versions of the spelling of names of Nootka chieftains versions will be used in direct quotations; otherwise these important personages will be called Maquinna, Natzape, and Tlupananulg.

26 Suria, *Voyage*, pp. 74-5.

27 Suria, *Voyage*, p. 75.

28 Suria, *Voyage*, p. 77.

29 In Apuntes, Noticias y correspondencias pertenecientes a la Expedicion de Malaspina, MS 427 in Museo Naval.

30 Apuntes, Noticias y correspondencias pertenecientes a la Expedicion de Malaspina, MS 427 in Museo Naval; and Suria, *Voyage*, p. 77.

31 The Spanish explorers customarily used the term rancheria to denote native villages. This has brought the term into English language usage.

32 Unless otherwise indicated the account of the Espinosa-Cevallos reconnaissance is based on Viaje en Limpio de las Corbetas Descubierta y Atrevida, MS 181 in Museo Naval. An alternate version appears in Corbetas, tomo III, MS 92 bis, in Museo Naval.

33 Viaje al Estrecho de Fuca, tomo II, MS 144 in Museo Naval.

34 Tova, *62 Meses a bordo*, p. 166.

35 Viaje en Limpio de las Corbetas Descubierta y Atrevida, MS 181 in Museo Naval.

36 "Examen político de las Costas N.O. de la América," manuscript in the hand of Malaspina, in California y Costa N.O. de América, tomo I, MS 330 in Museo Naval. Except for that statement, all of the information concerning the visit to Tahsis is contained in Viaje en Limpio de las Corbetas Descubierta y Atrevida, MS 181 in Museo Naval.

37 In another document Malaspina listed the items of treasure that Maquinna had at this time as being two glass windows, many implements of iron, an unspeakable quantity of trade beads, bottles, sheets of iron, etc.

38 Entry of 18 August in Libro de Guardias, Descubierta, MS 729 in Museo Naval.

39 Entry of 19 August in Libro de Guardias, Descubierta, MS 729 in Museo Naval.

40 Entry of 19 August in Libro de Guardias, Atrevida, MS 755 in Museo Naval.

41 Libro de Guardias, Atrevida, MS 755, original in Museo Naval, entry by Lieutenant Antonio Tova y Arredondo. This important officer merited the praise of the co-commander of the scientific exploring expedition, José Bustamante y Guerra, in the following terms: "In acquiring ethnographical information— religion, origin, government, commerce, geography – we cannot deny that the most essential part was taken by Antonio Tova, who making use of singular patience and methodology, combined with a moderate knowledge of the language, was able to obtain from his informants an understanding of his questions." José Bustamante y Guerra, Journal, MS, original in the Archivo del Ministerio de Relaciones Exteriores, Madrid, Manuscript 13, entry of 25 August 1791.

42 Malaspina, *Viaje científico y política...,* p. 310.

43 Tova, *62 Meses a bordo*, p. 165.

44 Suria, *Voyage*, pp. 75-6.

45 Secundino Salamanca in Libro de Guardias, Descubierta, MS 729 in Museo Naval.

46 Tova, *62 Meses a bordo*, p. 165. One of the journalists indicated that such sponsors had to be married, and indicated that the number of twenty-two included those already transported to San Blas and those who were on the point of being sent there in 1791.

47 Tova, *62 Meses a bordo*, p. 165.

48 Although he is mentioned as an old man, Tlupananulg could hardly have been over 45 years old.

49 Suria, *Voyage*, pp. 76-7.

50 Entry by Tova in Libro de Guardias, Atrevida, MS 755 in Museo Naval. It is perhaps this song which was recorded by the versatile naturalist, Tadeo Haenke, the fragment of which is preserved in the Museo Naval.

51 23 August in Libro de Guardias, Descubierta, MS 729 in Museo Naval. Tomás Suria drew a pencil sketch of Tlupananulg, as well as of the war canoe of that chief. On the following day, 24 August, Tlupananulg ordered his people to dance again, apparently this time on the beach near the observatory which had been set up for gravitational and astronomical calculations. Suria captured that scene in a rough sketch which was subsequently made into a finished copy, both of which are in the Museo Naval.

52 Tova, *62 Meses a bordo*, p. 169.

53 Entry of 25 August in Libro de Guardias, Atrevida, MS 755 in Museo Naval.

54 Disjointed notes in the hand of Alejandro Malaspina, MS, in Virreinato de Mexico, tomo I, MS 567 in Museo Naval.

55 Viaje al Estrecho de Fuca, tomo II, MS 144 in Museo Naval.

56 Obtained on various occasions from several sources, and sometimes containing seemingly contradictory information, the material presented in this chapter is as the Spaniards recorded it, save for its translation into English. Modern ethnologists will be in a position of comparing these early Spanish comments with other contemporary information and with Nootka tradition as obtained at a later date.

57 Entry of 27 August in Libro de Guardias, Atrevida, MS 755 in Museo Naval.

58 These were the British vessels *Ifigenia Nubiana* and *Argonaut*, under William Douglas (1788) and James Colnett (1789), respectively; and the United States vessels *Columbia* and *Lady Washington*, under John Kendrick and Robert Gray, both of which wintered on the Northwest Coast in 1788-1789.

59 "Examen político de las Costas N.O. de la America," in California y Coast N.O. de América, tomo I, MS 330 in Museo Naval.

60 Francisco Xavier de Viana, *Diario del Teniente de Navío D. Francisco Xavier de Viana, trabajado en el viaje de las corbetas de S.M.C. "Descubierta" y "Atrevida," en los años de 1789, 1790, 1791, 1792 y 1793* (Cerrito de la Victoria, Uruguay, 1849), p. 224.

61 González, *Tratado de enfermedades*, p. 79.

62 Bustamante, Journal, MS 13 in Archivo del Ministerio de Asuntos Exteriores, Madrid.

63 Malaspina, *Viaje científico y político...*, p. 314.

64 Viana, *Diario*, pp. 222-24.

65 Malaspina, *Viaje científico y político...*, p. 314.

66 Letter of Malaspina to Conde de Revilla Gigedo, Acapulco, 14 December 1791 in Archivo Histórico Nacional, Estado 4288. In the earlier instructions to Espinosa and Cevallos for their navigation of the interior canals at Nootka they were instructed to leave buried some coins and in "a bottle the notices of the exploration with the date on which it was carried out: These will be the only evidences of our possession and will be noted in the diary...," Apuntes, Noticias y correspondencia pertenecientes a la Expedición de Malaspina, MS 427 in Museo Naval.

67 A drawing of this titled "Caxon donde entra el Gefe de Nutka a sus supersticiones [Box where the Chief of Nootka enters for his superstitious rites]" was drawn by Cardero. It was later used in the publication of the voyage of the *Sutil* and *Mexicana* as plate No. 15, but with the subtitle of "Caxon u Oratorio del Tays de Nutka." The drawing might have been done in 1791 but more probably in 1792.

68 "Noticias que nos dió Maquina" in California y Costa N.O. de América, tomo I, MS 330 in Museo Naval. Most of the document concerns activities of the following year, 1792.

69 Virreinato de Mexico, tomo I, MS 567 in Museo Naval.

70 Engstrand (ed.), *Noticias de Nutka,* p. 63.

71 Alejandro Malaspina, Examen político de las costas de N.O. de la América, in California y Costa N.O. de América, tomo I, MS 330 in Museo Naval.

72 According to the visitors, the abalone at that earlier time were destined normally for eating purposes and at times for adornment. The price grew disproportionately larger when they were of greater size, and they were considered of valuable size when the circumference of the shell reached three *jemes*, an ancient informal and imprecise Spanish measurement involving the distance between the forefinger and the thumb, both fingers being extended, which would mean that the three jeme standard was about fifty centimetres.

73 In Reyno de Mexico, tomo III, MS 335 in the Museo Naval.

74 Viaje al Estrecho de Fuca, tomo II, MS 144 in Museo Naval.

75 Malaspina, "Extract...," in Reyno de Mexico, tomo III, MS 535 in Museo Naval.

76 Entry of 22 August in Libro de Guardias, Descubierta, MS 729 in Museo Naval.

77 "Relación de los efectos de viveres..." Document 47 in Hacienda 479, Archivo General de la Nación.

78 The Reaumur scale, formulated by Rene Antoine Ferchault de Reaumur in the eighteenth century, has 80 degrees between freezing at 0 degrees and boiling.

79 Dr. González, in his *Tratado de enfermedades,* pp. 474-75 gives some detail on the manufacture of spruce and pine beer which was brewed from conifer leaves, brown sugar, either barley, oat or corn mash, mixed with ground biscuit or bread.

80 Malaspina, *Viaje científico y político...*, p. 310.

81 As summarized in an entry of 27 August 1791 by Ciriaco Cevallos in Libro de Guardias, Atrevida, MS 755 in Museo Naval.

82 Malaspina, *Viaje científico y político...*, p. 194.

83 A recapitulation of the summer's work in the Pacific Northwest is facilitated by the expedition methodology which called for periodic forwarding of items of interest back to Spain. From such listing a reasonably complete summary of the recently completed scientific study can be obtained. Following the Northwest Coast phase (and including the stay in California), the following manifest resulted:

Note of what the present shipment to Madrid from the corvettes *Descubierta* and *Atrevida* contains:
Two drawings of scenes at Port Desengaño done by Ravenet and Brambila.
Diary of the latest navigation from Acapulco to the Northwest Coast of America until return to said port.
Astronomical diary of the same voyage, including the experiments with gravity with the simple fixed pendulum.
Meteorological diary of the same voyage.
Summary of magnetic variations.
Physical description of the coasts explored north of Cape Blanco in 43° 0'.

Political examination of the same [coasts].

Drawings by Don Tomás Suria and Josef Cardero of the most important objects during the last campaign. Glass has been placed over those that have been done in pencil so that they do not become erased. Some are missing, which are being made into completed copies by Suria.

Box No. 15. Collection of artifacts of all kinds from Port Mulgrave. A large canoe of *tinaja* (?) will be sent from Manila.

Box No. 16. The same collection from Nootka, and sea otter skins from different latitudes.

Box No. 17. The same collection from Monterey, and stuffed birds [from the Northwest Coast and California].

Box No. 18. A bundle of bows and arrows from the ports visited.

Note: If boxes No. 15 and 16 are to be opened, precautions should be taken against the disagreeable odour of the sea lion and whale oil, which it has not been possible to remove completely.

The detailed explanation of the things contained in those boxes and in No. 17 is in Box No. 18.

In addition, though not listed on this shipment, there were three "spherical" charts; five maps (Mulgrave, Desengaño, Nootka, Monterey and San Blas); and a notebook of rough sketches of the coast from all the last campaign.

ALCALA GALIANO AND THE 1792 RECONNAISSANCE

1 Francisco Antonio Mourelle, born in Galicia, had come up the hard way to his commissioned officer status. He was not an academy graduate, but rather had his training at the Spanish pilotage school of San Telmo in Seville. Although from that background the jump to commissioned officer status was not totally impossible, it was difficult to make the transition. Mourelle not only did so, he eventually became a flag rank officer, was frequently decorated, and in death at age 65 in 1820 was buried in the Pantheon of Illustrious Mariners at San Fernando near Cádiz. Additional detail on his life is found in Cutter, "California, Training Ground for Spanish Naval Heroes," in California Historical Society *Quarterly*, Vol. XXXX, No. 2 (June 1961), pp. 109-14, 120.

2 Although the voyage of the *Sutil* and *Mexicana* has been considered to have been under the overall command of Dionisio Alcalá Galiano, the contemporary documentation makes it clear that the two officers were at the time considered to be co-commanders. By naval protocol this is as it should have been, since they were promoted to commander with the same date of rank. Two factors may have been responsible for Alcalá Galiano getting top billing: 1) he was senior in age to Cayetano Valdés; and 2) he may have been the author of the *Relación* of the 1792 voyage. In the latter regard, it is almost certain that Valdés was not responsible for creation of the contemporary account.

3 Alcalá Galiano to Pedro de Varela, Madrid, 27 November 1795 in Malaspina, 1788-1814, MS 2296 in Museo Naval.

4 Malaspina's instructions dated 14 December 1791 at Acapulco are found in Archivo Histórico Nacional, Estado 4288.

5 Estado...[de] la Goleta...Mexicana...Acapulco, 8 March 1792 and Estado...[de] la Goleta...Sutil...Acapulco, 8 March 1792 in Archivo General de la Nación, Historia 558.

6 "Noticias que nos dió Maquina," in California y Costa N.O. de América, MS 330 in Museo Naval.

7 California y Costa N.O. de América, tomo I, MS 330 in Museo Naval. An abbreviated version of this visit to Malvinas is contained in the Relacion del Viaje.

8 California y Costa N.O. de América, tomo I, MS 330 in Museo Naval. Much of the information contained in Salamanca's inquiry was the result of the 1792 visit, though some information reflects the earlier visit of 1791. This dual use of information makes today's identification of sources difficult. He admits that a great deal of what he had to say about Nootka was borrowed from José Mariano Moziño, the natural scientist who was there in 1792 with Bodega y Quadra. The entire story of the voyage of the *Sutil* and *Mexicana* is complicated by failure to come to a positive identification of the author thereof, and by the existence of several nearly identical manuscript versions of the actual voyage. It seems most likely that Cardero, by the nature of his position, was the person most capable of carrying out the duty of journalist, but this fact does not guarantee that the ideas incorporated were his, either solely or principally.

9 Only one published account resulted and it was clearly a reduced version of what was originally written. Lengthy speculation concerning the author of the published account is contained in *California in 1792: Report of a Spanish Naval Visit*. Briefly summarized, it indicates that we will never know positively who wrote the journal, but that José Cardero seems the most logical person. The published report is quite brief compared to the time spent, and only rarely does it indicate that illustrations were being made of events and personages involved. The multiple drawings done by Cardero amplify and, in great measure, surpass the written comments. At the same time, they are most helpful in tracing the events of the voyage. The same can be said for the maps. Combining these sources, it is possible to recreate the long trip in a sketchy way.

10 Also drawn by Cardero, but labeled by some one else, was a "Fortification of the Indians of the Strait of Fuca." This has not been positively identified, and there is no certainty that it was a native fortification. The background does not give enough detail to pinpoint the area, not even as regards on which side of the strait the fortification was located, though it was probably on the south shore.

11 The translation is from Henry R. Wagner, *Spanish Explorations in the Strait of Juan de Fuca* (New York, 1971), pp. 221-22. The account of this activity is from the extract of the voyage, rather than from the diary.

12 Wagner, *Spanish Explorations in the Strait of Juan de Fuca*, p. 222.

13 It is doubtful that any expedition comments concerning Nootka resulted from that brief and busy stopover.

EPILOGUE

1. Malaspina's promotion to brigadier was dated 24 March 1795 and issued at Aranjuez, folio 190, Malaspina, 1788-1814, MS 2296 in Museo Naval.

Sources and Bibliography on Malaspina

Much archival material concerning the expedition was self-generated, official and semi-official documentation. Supplementary biographical information comes from a variety of sources, mostly navy personnel records. Archives in the Americas hold very little pertinent material, as there was no logical need for places visited by Malaspina to report on the expedition's activity. He was the reporter; they were the subjects of his inquiry. One exception to the general rule of things being official was the private journal or journals kept by expedition artist Tomás de Suria, who was not encouraged to engage in such activity. He felt that much information was purposely kept from him. There is no way of knowing the truth, but it would not have been in the expedition's best interest to have an authoritative version ready for premature publication, as would have been the case of Suria making his potentially fulsome journal of one phase of the exploring expedition available nearly three years before conclusion of that enterprise.

Suria interspersed his journal with rough sketches, many of which he later finished. The temporary artist's account lacks some of the maritime jargon of other versions, and it focuses on and therefore magnifies Suria's contribution. But, it has the freshness and naiveté of a landlubber's impression of seaboard activity. This independent view is refreshing when placed beside the highly repetitive official and semi-official versions written by men who were able to check notes and to verify what they said by reference to the official log. For example, an early August storm that only warranted a few lines in the official accounts is in Suria's journal converted into a raging tempest from which the expedition barely escaped, the recounting of which took a great deal of space.

Other sources, and only when in port, were the daily entries of the officer of the day in the Libros de Guardia (guard books). Daily watch duty done on a rotational basis by the commissioned officers and midshipmen resulted in notes which were contemporary with the events recorded, usually entered at the end of the regulation twenty-four-hour period. Such guard books are the only existing source of some information, such as disciplinary action, departure and return of personnel, absence without leave, and loading or unloading operations. The guard book notations, when consulted in conjunction with other accounts, frequently make the latter more intelligible.

The expedition chaplains kept a record particularly noting if each expedition member fulfilled his yearly church obligation of confession and communion, a duty normally performed during the Easter season. This comes the closest of any document to being a roll of the expedition members, but it never seems complete. Notes at times indicated certain persons who were non-Catholics or non-Spaniards, and sometimes non-Spanish speaking. These records also detail the demise of any crew members in cases of deaths while at sea or when persons died in port before they could be sent off to the hospital. In such cases as were recorded, there is information concerning place of birth, names of parents, religious orientation, and plans for disposal of the personal property of the deceased.

Special logs were kept to record celestial observations, positions calculated therefrom, and other nautical information. Maps made by expedition working parties, both preliminary and finished versions, exist in the Museo Naval. Botanical and zoological information, often accompanied by specimens and/or illustrations, is found in the Archivo del Real Jardín Botánico and the Archivo del Museo de Ciencias Naturales, both in Madrid.

The official accounts form the heart of the expedition story, frequently being what Malaspina intended to say as the final word. This is therefore what Pedro de Novo y Colson included in his edition of *Viaje científico y político alrededor del mundo por las corbetas Descubierta y Atrevida* published in Madrid in 1885, almost one hundred years after it was originally written.

Parallel versions by expedition members have appeared. One by Francisco Xavier de Viana was published in Uruguay in 1849. Another account, by *Atrevida* executive officer Antonio de Tova Arredondo, was prepared for publication in 1943 [?] by Lorenzo San Feliu Ortiz. The original manuscript is in the Biblioteca Menéndez Pelayo in Santander.

A considerable legacy of source materials of the areas touched by Malaspina's voyage existed, forgotten in archives, private collections and government bureaus. Included were drawings done by artists Suria and Cardero, the coastal profiles, the specimens, many of the documents and most of the articles of native manufacture. For many years they reposed undisturbed, and Malaspina, in conformity with the sentence of his court martial, had become a non-person with his name virtually unknown. After nearly a century the first step in recognition of Malaspina was taken by the aforementioned Novo y Colson with his edition of Malaspina's *Viaje científico y político*.... That single large volume contained much information, but it left much untouched, either for lack of space or because it was not available at that time.

More recently, appreciation of Malaspina and his work has gathered momentum. "Lost" documents have surfaced, specimens have been identified, drawings have been found and studied, and artifacts have been unpacked and displayed. So much has been done concerning the Pacific Northwest as to lead one modern Spanish scholar to comment that there is more of Nootka in Spain than there is of Spain in Nootka. Exhibits such as that held at the Vancouver Maritime Museum from January to April 1991, as well as the focus of recent research, not just on the exploratory activities of the late eighteenth century, but specifically on Malaspina's expedition, make this generalization somewhat less true. The temporary return of materials, among them some of the oldest extant artifacts, together with new publications, make that story live again to form part of the Pacific Northwest Coast's past – its Spanish heritage.

Art as a Source of Expedition Information

Diminishing artistic activity, compounded by a lack of versatility, motivated Malaspina to write to Europe for high-powered replacements. His Italian connections brought forth two new artists, but the impossibility of their intercepting the expedition before its departure for the Northwest Coast reduces their role in that campaign to a minimum, but does not make it totally nil. Expedition methodology permitted both to play a small role in the extant archive of early Northwest Coast art, since later they provided "improved" versions of earlier rough sketches. And some of these "improved" drawings were subject to even later final versions. One result of these alterations is the modern difficulty in ascribing authority for all drawings and the realization that the same scene or subject might be the work of two different artists. Of greater negative consequence is that the final artist took liberties in changing details to achieve stylistic effects or to suit his own interpretation of the scene or persons depicted, even if he had never seen them. Fortunately, many of the rough and intermediate sketches exist from which we can evaluate the amount of artistic license later taken.

As far as the Northwest Coast is concerned, the total artistic production was greatly enhanced by the emergence from humbler duties of an untrained artist. José Cardero, an original expedition member, had signed aboard the *Descubierta* as a cabin boy, but apparently possessed some talent in art. He subsequently became important not only to the Malaspina visit in 1791 but even more so to the visit of Alcalá Galiano and Valdés in 1792. The little servant of the officers was born in Ecija in Andalusia, and was self-taught, with the result that he drew as carefully as possible what he saw and that with practice he became increasingly able. For art historians Cardero is the least interesting, but for historians studying the expeditions, his fidelity to detail is an important bonus. If a wall had twenty courses of bricks, he drew twenty; if there were ten persons present, he drew exactly that number. Cardero's work is important on other counts as well, for he was the most prolific Northwest Coast artist visiting the area in both 1791 and 1792.

Suria, who outlived most members of the expedition, returned to Mexico City where after about one year spent finishing his drawings, an assignment requested by Malaspina, he returned to his position at the Casa de Moneda (the Mint) where he was an artist/engraver. His account was never published in his lifetime nor for many years thereafter.

Select Bibliography

Archives

Archivo General de la Nación, Mexico
    Hacienda 479
    Historia 558

Archivo Histórico Nacional, Madrid
    Estado 4288

Archivo del Museo de Ciencias Naturales, Madrid
    Pineda, Notas, 2 vols.

Archivo del Ministerio de Asuntos Exteriores, Madrid
    Manuscript 13

Museo Naval, Madrid
    Corbetas, tomo III, MS 92 bis
    Pacífico América, tomo I, MS 126
    Viaje al Estrecho de Fuca, tomo II, MS 144
    Viaje en Limpio de las Corbetas Descubierta y Atrevida, MS 181
    Descubierta y Atrevida, Observaciones, MS 264
    Malaspina Correspondencia, tomo II, MS 279
    Costa Oriental de la América Meridional en 1790, tomo V,
        MS 289
    California y Costa N.O. de América, tomo I, MS 330
    Costa N.O. de América, tomo II, MS 332
    Reyno de Mexico, tomo III, MS 335

Apuntes, Noticias y correspondencias pertenecientes a la
    Expedición de Malaspina, MS 427
Bauzá, Diario del viaje al rededor del mundo..., MS 479
Virreinato de Mexico, tomo I, MS 567
California, Historia y Viajes, tomo I, MS 575
Correspondencia relativa al viaje de Malaspina, tomo A, MS 583
Libro de Guardias, Descubierta, MS 729
Libro de Guardias, Atrevida, MS 755
Compañías de Guardias Marinas, Cádiz, MS 1073
Partida de Defunción y Testamento de Bauzá, MS 1821
[Untitled box of documents], MS 2513

Books

Beals, Herbert K. (trans. & ed.). *For Honor and Country: The Diary of Bruno De Hezeta.* Portland, 1985.

Cutter, Donald C. *Malaspina in California.* San Francisco, 1960.

_____ (ed.). *Journal of Tomás de Suria and His Voyage with Malaspina to the Northwest Coast of America in 1791.* Fairfield, Washington, 1980.

_____. *California in 1792: Report of a Spanish Naval Visit.* Norman, Oklahoma, 1990.

Destefani, Laurio H., and Donald Cutter. *Tadeo Haenke y el final de una vieja polémica.* Buenos Aires, 1966.

Dixon, George. *A Voyage round the world, but more particularly to the Northwest Coast of America.* London, 1789.

Engstrand, Iris II. Wilson (ed.). *Noticias de Nutka: An Account of Nootka Sound in 1792.* Seattle and London, 1970.

González, Pedro María. *Tratado de las enfermedades de la gente de mar, en que se exponen sus causas y los medios de precaverlas.* Madrid, 1805.

Higueras, Dolores, *Catálogo Crítico de los Documentos de las Expedición Malaspina*, Museo Naval, Madrid, 1985, 3 vols.

Laguna, Federica de. *Under Mount Saint Elias: The History and Culture of the Yakutat Tlingit.* Washington, D.C., 1972.

Malaspina, Alejandro. *Viaje científico y político alrededor del mundo por las corbetas Descubierta y Atrevida.* Edited by Pedro de Novo y Colson. Madrid, 1885.

Novo y Colson, Pedro de. *See*: Malaspina.

Palau, Mercedes, *Catálogo de los Dibujos, Aguadas y Acuarelas de la Expedición Malaspina*, 1789-1794, Museo de América, Madrid, 1980.

Relación del viaje hecho por las goletas Sutil y Mexicana en el año 1792. 2 vols, Madrid, 1802.

San Feliu Ortiz, Lorenzo (ed.), *62 Meses a bordo: La expedición Malaspina según el diario del Teniente de Navío Don Antonio de Tova Arredondo, 2° Comandante de la ATREVIDA, 1789-1794.* Madrid, 1943?.

Sotos, Carmen, *Los Pintores de la Expedición de Alejandro Malaspina*, Real Academia de la Histiria, Madrid, 1982, 2 vols.

Suria, Tomás de. *See*: Cutter.

Tova Arredondo, Antonio de. *See*: San Feliu Ortiz.

Viana, Francisco Xavier de. *Diario del Teniente de Navío D. Francisco Xavier de Viana...en los años de 1789, 1790, 1791, 1792 y 1793.* Cerrito de la Victoria, Uruguay, 1849.

Wagner, Henry R. *Spanish Exploration in the Strait of Juan de Fuca.* Reprint, New York 1971.

Articles

Cutter, Donald C. "The First American in California," *The Californians*, Vol. 1, No. 5 (September-October, 1983).

_____. "Pedro Alberni y los primeros experimentos de agricultura científica en la costa nordoeste de Pacífico," in *Revista de Historia Naval*, Año V, No. 18 (1987).

_____. "California: Training Ground for Spanish Naval Heroes," in California Historical Society *Quarterly*, Vol. XXXX, No. 2, (June 1961).

_____. "Las Dotaciones y la travesía," in *La Expedición Malaspina, 1789-1794: Viaje a América y Oceania de las Corbetas "Descubierta" y "Atrevida."* (Madrid, l984).

Galbraith, Edith C. "Malaspina's Voyage Around the World," California Historical Society *Quarterly*, Vol. III (1924).

Kandert, Joseph. "Catalogue of Ethnographical Collections of Tadéas Hanke," in *Annals of the Náprstek Museum 13* (Prague, 1985).

Index